BUTTERBALL

Turkey Lovers'
COOKBOOK

Publications International, Ltd.

Front cover photography (top row: second from left and far right; main photograph) and photographs on pages 11, 13, 15, 17, 19, 21, 23, 25, 27, 29, 31, 33, 35, 37, 41, 43, 44, 45, 47, 49, 50, 51, 53, 55, 56, 57, 59, 61, 63, 65, 67, 69, 71, 73, 74, 75, 76, 77, 79, 81, 83, 85, 87, 89, 90, 127, 129, 131, and 135 shot at Chris Cassidy Photography, Chicago.

Photographer: Chris Cassidy
Photographer's assistants: Annemarie Zelasko, Christy Clow
Food stylists: Josephine Orba, Cindy Melin, Kim Hartman
Food stylists' assistants: Lisa Knych, Marena Upton

Pictured on the front cover (left to right): Smoked Sausage with Mediterranean-Style Vegetables *(page 114)*, Smoked Sausage Frittata *(page 116)*, BLT Turkey Burger *(page 96)*, Open-Face Turkey Caprese Sandwich *(page 75)*, and Roast Turkey with Pan Juices *(page 10)*.

Pictured on the back cover (top to bottom): Turkey Pomodoro *(page 60)*, Soft Turkey Tacos *(page 91)*, Spicy Turkey with Citrus au Jus *(page 106)*, and Maple-Basted Roast Turkey with Cranberry Pan Gravy *(page 26)*.

ISBN-13: 978-1-4508-6600-2
ISBN-10: 1-4508-6600-x

Library of Congress Control Number: 2013930696

Manufactured in China.

8 7 6 5 4 3 2 1

Microwave Cooking: Microwave ovens vary in wattage. Use the cooking times as guidelines and check for doneness before adding more time.

contents

BUTTERBALL®

Turkey Lovers' COOKBOOK

When you hear the name "Butterball," you probably imagine the enticing aromas of Thanksgiving dinner—pumpkin pies cooling on the counter, side dishes galore, and, of course, a stuffed turkey roasting to perfection in the oven. This cherished holiday is one that overflows with memorable moments and mouthwatering flavors.

Since 1954, when we introduced the first Butterball turkey, we've seen just how much America loves our tender and juicy turkeys at Thanksgiving. But we've also seen that people love turkey no matter what the occasion, whether as the star of the perfect summer sandwich or as a better-for-you breakfast choice.

So, we've compiled some of our best recipes to show you how easy it is to savor the delicious flavor and consistent high quality of Butterball turkey throughout the year.

In these pages, you'll find plenty of reasons to bring family and friends together to celebrate with turkey every day. Our great-tasting turkey dishes, side dishes, and even desserts, such as Cake and Ice Cream "Pops" and Southern Pecan Pie with Toffee Crunch, are just what your taste buds are looking for.

We've even included useful information about cooking methods, food-safety guidelines, and tips from our Certified Master Chef to help you in the kitchen.

Now there's no reason to wait for the holidays, because Butterball makes meals better every day—these recipes mean turkey is yours to enjoy any day of the week, starting tonight!

tips for the *perfect turkey*

At Butterball, we know turkey—after all, we've been selling Butterball turkeys for nearly 60 years. And, for more than 30 years, our Turkey Talk-Line® experts have been sharing advice about cooking the perfect turkey. Here's a collection of our best and most requested tips.

Thawing

Before you start cooking, safe and complete thawing is an essential step to make sure your turkey is cooked to perfection.

Refrigerator thawing: Thaw your turkey in its unopened wrapper on a shallow tray. Allow at least 1 day of thawing for every 4 pounds of turkey. Check to make sure your refrigerator is no warmer than 40°F.

Net Weight	Thaw Time
7 to 10 lbs.	2 to 3 days
10 to 18 lbs.	3 to 4 days
18 to 22 lbs.	4 to 5 days
22 to 24 lbs.	5 to 6 days
24 to 30 lbs.	6 to 7 days
Bone-in Breast	1 to 2 days
Roasts	1½ to 2 days
Butterball Baked Turkey	2 to 5 days
Butterball Smoked Turkey	2 to 4 days

Cold-water thawing: To hasten thawing, you can thaw a whole turkey in its unopened wrapper, breast side down, in a sink or large container of cold tap water. Allow about 30 minutes for every 1 pound of turkey. Change the water every 30 minutes to hasten the process.

Net Weight	Thaw Time
8 to 12 lbs.	4 to 6 hours
12 to 16 lbs.	6 to 8 hours
16 to 20 lbs.	8 to 10 hours
20 to 24 lbs.	10 to 12 hours
24 to 30 lbs.	12 to 15 hours
Bone-in Breast	4 to 8 hours
Roasts	3 to 5 hours

Cooking Methods

Open-pan method: The open-pan cooking method will result in a tender and juicy turkey with a golden-brown appearance and a rich, roasted flavor.

1. Preheat the oven to 325°F.

2. Use a shallow, open roasting pan about 2½ inches deep.

3. Thaw and prepare the turkey according to the package or recipe instructions.

4. Place the turkey, breast side up, on a flat rack in the bottom of the roasting pan.

5. For better appearance, brush the skin with vegetable oil before roasting. (You may use nonstick cooking spray instead.) Don't add any liquid to the pan. Don't cover the pan.

6. Place it in the preheated oven.

7. To prevent overcooking the breast, loosely cover the breast and the top of the drumsticks with foil when the turkey is about two-thirds done.

Continued on page 6.

Continued from page 5.

8. Insert an oven-safe food thermometer deep into the lower part of the thigh muscle, but make sure it is not touching the bone. If the turkey is stuffed, when the thigh reaches the correct temperature, move the thermometer to the center of the stuffing to ensure the stuffing also has reached the correct temperature.

9. The turkey is done when the meat thermometer reaches the following temperatures:

- 180°F deep in the thigh; also, when the thigh muscle is pierced deeply, the juices should be clear, not reddish pink;
- 165°F in the center of the stuffing, if the turkey is stuffed;
- 170°F in the breast.

Net Weight	Thawed / Fresh (40°F) Roast Time (Stuffed)	Thawed / Fresh (40°F) Roast Time (Unstuffed)
4½ to 7 lbs.	2¼ to 2¾ hours	2 to 2½ hours
7 to 10 lbs.	2¾ to 3½ hours	2½ to 3 hours
10 to 18 lbs.	3¾ to 4½ hours	3 to 3½ hours
18 to 22 lbs.	4½ to 5 hours	3½ to 4 hours
22 to 24 lbs.	5 to 5½ hours	4 to 4½ hours
24 to 30 lbs.	5½ to 6¼ hours	4½ to 5 hours
Boneless Breast Roasts	n/a	1¾ to 2 hours (2½ to 3 hours from frozen state)
Bone-in Breasts	2 to 3¼ hours	1½ to 2¾ hours

Approximate roasting times for whole turkeys (fresh or thawed turkeys, refrigerated at 40°F or less) when roasted in a conventional oven preheated to 325°F, and placed breast side up on a flat rack in a shallow uncovered roasting pan. For best results, always check for doneness using a meat thermometer; if stuffed, check the stuffing temperature too.

- ***Deep-frying method:*** For the best results, use the Butterball Indoor Electric Turkey Deep Fryer (for turkeys weighing up to 14 lbs.) or the XL model (for larger turkeys weighing up to 20 lbs.). This deep fryer offers cooks a safe and easy way to prepare a golden deep-fried turkey any time of year.

  Follow the directions to preheat the oil to the correct temperature. Place the turkey into the basket, breast side up, and lower the basket into the hot oil. Fry for 3½ to 4 minutes per pound. Make sure you unplug the fryer before removing the turkey. For moist meat, let the turkey rest in the fryer basket 10 minutes before carving.

- ***Oven-bag method:*** Add flour to the bag and shake to coat the inside of the bag. Arrange the bag on a shallow pan. Add your favorite vegetables, such as sliced onions and celery. Place the turkey in the bag, breast side up, on top of the vegetables. Close the bag, cut slits into it, and bake the turkey at 350°F for the amount of time recommended by the bag manufacturer's chart.

Food Safety Tips

- Keep all cold food below 40°F (including a fresh or thawed turkey) and all hot food above 140°F to keep foods safe to eat.

- Fully cooking poultry—and any stuffing—to a minimum of 165°F destroys bacteria that could cause food-borne illness.

- While thawing a turkey, prevent any uncooked juices from dripping onto other foods in the refrigerator. Place the packaged turkey on a separate tray or in a sealed dish on the bottom shelf of the refrigerator. (See the chart on page 5 for thawing times, based on the weight of your turkey.)

- To prevent the possibility of any cross-contamination, store any raw turkey away from cooked meats, fresh fruit, and fresh vegetables.

- A thawed turkey may be kept in the refrigerator up to 4 days before it must be cooked.

- Cook a fresh turkey as soon as possible, but no later than the use-by date on the package.

- Use paper towels, not cloth, to wipe off the turkey and clean up any spilled juices; discard the paper towels.

- Wash your hands and any work surfaces and utensils touched by raw meat or poultry and its juices with hot, soapy water.

- Wash cutting boards thoroughly in hot, soapy water after each use. Allow the cutting boards to air dry or dry them with clean paper towels. Never mix raw and cooked foods on the same cutting board without washing the board first.

- Stuff the turkey just before roasting it, not the night before. If you prefer shorter turkey roasting times (see the chart on page 6), cook or bake the stuffing separately.

- Use cooking or roasting methods that allow a whole turkey to reach an internal temperature of 140°F in less than 4 hours and a final temperature of 180°F in the thigh. If stuffed, the stuffing should reach 165°F. Avoid using a roasting temperature lower than 325°F or a partial-cooking method.

- When roasting, use a meat thermometer to determine the turkey's doneness, as well as the temperature of the stuffing. If you don't have a meat thermometer to measure the internal temperature of the stuffing in the turkey, cook or bake the stuffing separately.

- Store the turkey, stuffing, gravy, broth, and other leftover cooked foods in separate containers in the refrigerator. Cover the containers tightly to protect the foods.

- Store cooked, carved turkey in the refrigerator as soon as your meal is over. The maximum time limit for keeping cooked meat at room temperature is 2 hours. Remove the turkey meat from the bones before storing.

Reheating Leftovers

Sometimes the best part of your turkey dinner is having leftovers. Leftover turkey can be used in so many different recipes—or reheated and served with gravy and stuffing, just like your holiday dinner.

- **Delicious, safe leftovers start with proper storage.** Always finish carving the meat off the bone before wrapping the meat in plastic wrap or aluminum foil, and refrigerating or freezing it for use in other recipes. Wings, thighs, and legs can be left whole, if desired. Wrap them separately, and refrigerate or freeze.

- **To reheat sliced turkey,** overlap slices and boned meat in a shallow layer in an ovenproof or microwave-safe dish. To keep it moist, sprinkle a little turkey or chicken broth over the meat or spoon on gravy, if desired.

- **To reheat in a conventional oven,** cover the dish with foil, and heat at 350°F for 35 minutes or until hot (140° to 150°F).

- **To reheat in a microwave oven,** cover the dish with plastic wrap and microwave at MEDIUM-HIGH (70% power) for 10 minutes or until hot (140° to 150°F).

- **To reheat turkey wings, thighs, or legs,** place the whole pieces in a single layer in a baking pan. Sprinkle them with turkey pan drippings or broth, and cover the pan with aluminum foil. Heat at 350°F for 40 minutes or until hot (140° to 150°F).

Health and Nutrition

Butterball continues to give cooks a reason to incorporate turkey year-round by offering better-for-you meal ideas and products that are packed with protein, are often gluten-free, and have the taste you love. These include:

- **Butterball Fully Cooked Turkey Bacon,** which has 65 percent less fat than pork bacon.

- **Butterball Original Deli** items, a great low-fat, lower-sodium option in the deli case.

- **Butterball Frozen Turkey Burgers,** which offer two-thirds of the daily recommended value for protein in one serving.

- **Butterball Turkey Dinner Sausages,** which offer 60 percent less fat than regular pork or beef smoked sausage.

- **Butterball Whole Turkeys,** which are all-natural, hormone-free, and gluten-free—delivering a tender and juicy turkey every time!

Tips From Master Chef Tony Seta

1. Don't pack your stuffing or dressing tightly into the turkey—it must be loosely packed to reach the temperature of 165°F before the turkey is overcooked.

2. Brush the turkey skin with dry vermouth soon after removing it from the oven to give the roasted skin an attractive shiny brown color.

3. Remove the roasted turkey from the oven, cover it with a sheet of foil, and let it rest 30 minutes before carving. The resting period helps the juices settle for moist meat and makes the turkey easier to carve.

4. Soak raw turkey tenderloins or breast cuts in buttermilk to add tenderness and moistness to the cooked meat.

5. Purchase cranberries that are hard (a fresh cranberry will bounce) and with colors that range from light to dark red. Remember to cook them only until they pop.

6. Always store potatoes in a cool dark area—do not refrigerate. Refrigeration turns some of the potato starch into sugar, causing dark spots on the potatoes when they're cooked.

7. Russet and Yukon Gold potatoes are two of the best potato varieties for mashed potatoes.

8. Peel potatoes the day before cooking them to save time when you're entertaining. To keep the peeled potatoes from discoloring, store them in a tightly sealed gallon-size plastic food storage bag filled with water and the juice of ½ lemon.

At Butterball, every recipe from our kitchen is developed with the help of our talented Certified Master Chef, Anthony (Tony) Seta. Chef Seta is one of only 62 Certified Master Chefs in the United States—an accomplishment that is only achieved through a rigorous testing process that combines a thorough knowledge of food, food preparation skills, and creativity.

Successfully developing creative and signature items for the restaurant and foodservice industry for more than 25 years, Chef Seta applies his expert food knowledge, innovative flavors, and love of turkey when developing recipes for Butterball.

He is a part of creating new recipes, testing new trends, and developing innovative meal solutions with an array of Butterball turkey products that will ensure your family has a delicious meal.

9. When preparing mashed potatoes, substitute buttermilk for milk to give them more buttery flavor.

10. To prevent salt stains on your cookware, don't add salt until the contents are boiling.

11. Soak wooden skewers in oil rather than water for easier kabob preparation and to prevent possible splintering.

12. For easy peeling, soak garlic in hot-to-the-touch water for about 30 minutes before peeling.

13. When sautéing ingredients that include garlic, start with the garlic. Sauté it 30 to 40 seconds or until the aroma of garlic fills the air, then quickly add the rest of your ingredients. If you accidently burn the garlic, start over—or you'll never lose the burned flavor.

Go beyond your traditional turkey recipe and experiment with new flavors—you'll find something to please every palate

The .
main *event*

Roast Turkey with Pan Juices

PREP 20 minutes **COOK** 3½ to 3¾ hours

- **1 (12- to 14-pound) BUTTERBALL® Fresh or Frozen Whole Turkey, thawed if frozen**
- **1 Granny Smith apple, peeled and cut into 1-inch pieces**
- **1 small onion, cut into quarters**
- **2 carrots, cut into 1-inch pieces**
- **2 stalks celery, cut into 1-inch pieces**
- **5 sprigs fresh sage**
- **5 sprigs fresh thyme**
- **Vegetable oil**
- **3 cups fat-free chicken broth**

1. Preheat oven to 325°F. Remove neck and giblets from body and neck cavities of turkey. Refrigerate for another use or discard. Pat turkey dry with paper towels. Turn wings back to hold neck skin in place. Place apple, onion, carrots, celery, sage and thyme in body cavity. Return legs to tucked position. Place turkey, breast side up, on flat rack in shallow roasting pan. Brush breast and legs lightly with oil.

2. Roast turkey 1½ hours. Then, cover breast and top of drumsticks loosely with aluminum foil to prevent overcooking.

3. Continue roasting turkey 1½ to 2 hours* or until meat thermometer reaches 180°F when inserted into deepest part of thigh not touching bone.

4. Transfer turkey to cutting board. Transfer apple, vegetables and herbs from body cavity to roasting pan. Loosely tent turkey with foil while preparing pan juices.

5. Place roasting pan on burners over medium heat. Bring to a boil, stirring to scrape browned bits from bottom of pan. Stir in broth; bring to a boil. Reduce heat to medium-low; simmer 20 minutes, skimming excess fat from mixture. Remove from heat. Strain mixture through fine-mesh sieve before serving with turkey.

*Follow cooking times according to package directions; times vary with size of turkey.

Makes 10 to 12 servings

Citrus Marinated Moroccan Roast Turkey

PREP 10 minutes   **MARINATE** 3 hours   **CHILL** 4 hours   **COOK** 3 to 3½ hours

TURKEY

- 1 (12- to 14-pound) BUTTERBALL® Fresh or Frozen Whole Turkey, thawed if frozen

CITRUS MARINADE

- 2 cups fresh orange juice
- 1 cup fresh lemon juice

RUB

- ¾ cup olive oil
- 2 tablespoons smoked paprika
- 2 tablespoons honey
- 1½ tablespoons minced garlic
- 1½ tablespoons minced fresh ginger
- 1 tablespoon ground coriander
- 1 tablespoon roasted ground cumin
- 1 teaspoon black pepper
- ½ teaspoon ground nutmeg
- ½ teaspoon red pepper flakes
- 2 oranges, cut into quarters
- 1 cup thinly sliced onions

GLAZE

- ½ cup pomegranate molasses, divided

1. Remove neck and giblets from body and neck cavities of turkey. Refrigerate for another use or discard. Pat turkey dry with paper towels. Place turkey, breast side down, in brining container or bag. Pour orange and lemon juices over turkey. Cover or seal bag; refrigerate 3 hours, turning turkey over occasionally.

2. Combine oil, paprika, honey, garlic, ginger, coriander, cumin, black pepper, nutmeg and red pepper flakes in blender or food processor. Process until smooth.

3. Remove turkey from juice; discard juice. Pat turkey dry with paper towels. Turn wings back to hold neck skin against back of turkey. Return legs to tucked position, if untucked. Place turkey, breast side up, on large pan. Apply prepared spice mixture onto turkey skin. Cover turkey; refrigerate at least 4 hours or overnight.

4. Preheat oven to 325°F. Place turkey, breast side up, on flat rack in shallow roasting pan. Place oranges and onions in body cavity. Return legs to tucked position.

5. Roast turkey 1½ hours. Then, cover breast and top of drumsticks loosely with aluminum foil to prevent overcooking.

6. Continue roasting turkey 1 hour. Uncover turkey breast and brush with ¼ cup molasses. Cover breast with foil and continue roasting turkey 30 minutes to 1 hour* or until meat thermometer reaches 180°F when inserted into deepest part of thigh not touching bone.

7. Transfer turkey to cutting board; brush with remaining ¼ cup molasses and loosely tent with foil. Let stand 15 minutes before carving. Remove and discard oranges and onions.

*Follow cooking times according to package directions; times vary with size of turkey.

Makes 10 to 12 servings

Apple Cider Marinated Roast Turkey

PREP 10 minutes **MARINATE** 6 to 8 hours **COOK** 3 to 3½ hours

APPLE CIDER MARINADE

- 1 **cup apple cider**
- ⅓ **cup apple jack brandy**
- ¼ **cup firmly packed dark brown sugar**
- ¼ **cup fresh lemon juice**
- 3 **tablespoons kosher salt**
- 2 **tablespoons chopped fresh sage**
- 1 **tablespoon chopped fresh rosemary**
- 1 **tablespoon crushed black peppercorns**
- 1 **teaspoon dry mustard**
- 3 **bay leaves**

TURKEY

- 1 **(12- to 14-pound) BUTTERBALL® Fresh or Frozen Whole Turkey, thawed if frozen**
- **Nonstick cooking spray**

1. Combine cider, brandy, brown sugar, lemon juice, salt, sage, rosemary, pepper, mustard and bay leaves in large nonmetallic container; stir until sugar is dissolved.

2. Remove neck and giblets from body and neck cavities of turkey. Refrigerate for another use or discard. Pat turkey dry with paper towels. Place turkey, breast side down, in marinade. Cover; refrigerate 6 to 8 hours, turning turkey over occasionally.

3. Preheat oven to 325°F. Remove turkey from marinade; discard marinade. Pat turkey dry with paper towels. Turn wings back to hold neck skin against back of turkey. Return legs to tucked position, if untucked. Place turkey, breast side up, on flat rack in shallow roasting pan; coat with cooking spray.

4. Roast turkey 1½ hours. Then, cover breast and top of drumsticks loosely with aluminum foil to prevent overcooking.

5. Continue roasting turkey 1½ to 2 hours* or until meat thermometer reaches 180°F when inserted into deepest part of thigh not touching bone.

6. Transfer turkey to cutting board; loosely tent with foil. Let stand 15 minutes before carving.

Follow cooking times according to package directions; times vary with size of turkey.

Makes 10 to 12 servings

Roast Turkey with Moroccan Rub

PREP 15 minutes   **CHILL** 2 to 4 hours   **COOK** 3 to 3½ hours

MOROCCAN RUB

- 1 tablespoon coriander seeds
- 1 tablespoon mustard seeds
- 1 dried Anaheim chile pepper
- 2 teaspoons cracked pink peppercorns
- 2 teaspoons cumin seeds
- 10 cardamom pods
- 8 whole cloves
- 1 star anise
- ½ bay leaf
- ¼ cup firmly packed dark brown sugar
- 2 teaspoons roasted ground cinnamon
- 1 teaspoon minced dried garlic
- 1 teaspoon ground ginger
- 1 teaspoon kosher salt
- 1 teaspoon dried thyme
- ½ teaspoon ground turmeric

TURKEY

- 1 (12- to 14-pound) BUTTERBALL® Fresh or Frozen Whole Turkey, thawed if frozen
- Vegetable oil

1. Place coriander seeds, mustard seeds, chile, pepper, cumin seeds, cardamom, cloves and star anise in heavy skillet over medium-high heat. Toast spices, swirling pan 2 to 3 minutes or until spices become fragrant. Transfer to plate; cool completely on wire rack.

2. Place toasted spices and bay leaf into spice grinder or small food processor. Process until finely ground. Transfer to small bowl; stir in brown sugar, cinnamon, garlic, ginger, salt, thyme and turmeric.

3. Remove neck and giblets from body and neck cavities of turkey. Refrigerate for another use or discard. Pat turkey dry with paper towels. Turn wings back to hold neck skin in place. Return legs to tucked position, if untucked. Place turkey, breast side up, on flat rack in shallow roasting pan. Brush breast and legs lightly with oil. Apply prepared rub on turkey skin; refrigerate 2 to 4 hours.

4. Preheat oven to 325°F. Roast turkey 1½ hours. Then, cover breast and top of drumsticks loosely with aluminum foil to prevent overcooking.

5. Continue roasting turkey 1½ to 2 hours* or until meat thermometer reaches 180°F when inserted into deepest part of thigh not touching bone.

6. Transfer turkey to cutting board; loosely tent with foil. Let stand 15 minutes before carving.

Follow cooking times according to package directions; times vary with size of turkey.

Makes 10 to 12 servings

<u>*tip*</u>

The Moroccan Rub mixture can be stored in an airtight container in a cool dry place for up to 3 weeks.

Bourbon and Cola Marinated Roast Turkey

PREP 5 minutes   **MARINATE** 6 to 8 hours   **COOK** 3 to 3½ hours

BOURBON AND COLA MARINADE

- ¾ **cup cola soda***
- ½ **cup bourbon**
- ⅓ **cup fresh lemon juice**
- ⅓ **cup soy sauce**
- ¼ **cup chopped green onion**
- 1 **tablespoon minced garlic**
- ½ **teaspoon crushed red pepper flakes**

TURKEY

- 1 **(12- to 14-pound) BUTTERBALL® Fresh or Frozen Whole Turkey, thawed if frozen**
- **Nonstick cooking spray**

*Do not use diet or low-calorie soda.

1. Combine soda, bourbon, lemon juice, soy sauce, green onion, garlic and red pepper flakes in large nonmetallic container; mix well.

2. Remove neck and giblets from body and neck cavities of turkey. Refrigerate for another use or discard. Pat turkey dry with paper towels. Place turkey, breast side down, in marinade. Cover; refrigerate 6 to 8 hours, turning turkey over occasionally.

3. Preheat oven to 325°F. Remove turkey from marinade; discard marinade. Pat turkey dry with paper towels. Turn wings back to hold neck skin against back of turkey. Return legs to tucked position, if untucked. Place turkey, breast side up, on flat rack in shallow roasting pan; coat with cooking spray.

4. Roast turkey 1½ hours. Then, cover breast and top of drumsticks loosely with aluminum foil to prevent overcooking.

5. Continue roasting turkey 1½ to 2 hours* or until meat thermometer reaches 180°F when inserted into deepest part of thigh not touching bone.

6. Transfer turkey to cutting board; loosely tent with foil. Let stand 15 minutes before carving.

*Follow cooking times according to package directions; times vary with size of turkey.

Makes 10 to 12 servings

Jamaican Rum, Pepper and Lime Marinated Turkey

PREP 20 minutes   **MARINATE** 6 to 8 hours   **COOK** 3 to 3½ hours

RUM MARINADE

- ¾ **cup prepared teriyaki sauce**
- ¾ **cup thinly sliced green onions**
- 2 **tablespoons grated lime peel**
- 2 **tablespoons grated orange peel**
- ½ **cup chili sauce**
- ⅓ **cup fresh lemon juice**
- ⅓ **cup fresh lime juice**
- ⅓ **cup dark rum**
- ⅓ **cup canola oil**
- ¼ **cup seeded finely chopped jalapeño peppers***
- ¼ **cup minced garlic**
- 3 **tablespoons jerk seasoning**
- 1 **tablespoon kosher salt**
- 1 **tablespoon cracked black peppercorns**

TURKEY

- 1 **(12- to 14-pound) BUTTERBALL® Fresh or Frozen Whole Turkey, thawed if frozen**
- **Nonstick cooking spray**

*Jalapeño peppers can sting and irritate the skin, so wear rubber gloves when handling peppers and do not touch your eyes.

1. Combine teriyaki sauce, green onions, lime peel, orange peel, chili sauce, lemon juice, lime juice, rum, oil, jalapeño peppers, garlic, seasoning, salt and pepper in large nonmetallic container; mix well.

2. Remove neck and giblets from body and neck cavities of turkey. Refrigerate for another use or discard. Pat turkey dry with paper towels. Place turkey, breast side down, in marinade. Cover; refrigerate 6 to 8 hours, turning turkey over occasionally.

3. Preheat oven to 325°F. Remove turkey from marinade; discard marinade. Pat turkey dry with paper towels. Turn wings back to hold neck skin against back of turkey. Return legs to tucked position, if untucked. Place turkey, breast side up, on flat rack in shallow roasting pan; coat with cooking spray.

4. Roast turkey 1½ hours. Then, cover breast and top of drumsticks loosely with aluminum foil to prevent overcooking.

5. Continue roasting turkey 1½ to 2 hours* or until meat thermometer reaches 180°F when inserted into deepest part of thigh not touching bone.

6. Transfer turkey to cutting board; loosely tent with foil. Let stand 15 minutes before carving.

Follow cooking times according to package directions; times vary with size of turkey.

Makes 10 to 12 servings

---

tip

This marinade adds great flavor when used on a turkey that will be cooked on a grill.

Honey and Spice Glazed Turkey

PREP 20 minutes   **COOK** 3 hours

HONEY AND SPICE GLAZE

- 2 teaspoons chili powder
- ½ teaspoon garlic powder
- ¼ teaspoon ground allspice
- ¼ teaspoon ground cumin
- ¼ teaspoon salt
- ⅛ teaspoon ground red pepper
- 2 tablespoons honey
- 1 teaspoon water

TURKEY

- 1 (14- to 16-pound) BUTTERBALL® Fresh or Frozen Whole Turkey, thawed if frozen
- Vegetable oil

1. Preheat oven to 325°F. Combine chili powder, garlic powder, allspice, cumin, salt, red pepper, honey and water in small bowl; mix well.

2. Remove neck and giblets from body and neck cavities of turkey. Refrigerate for another use or discard. Pat turkey dry with paper towels. Turn wings back to hold neck skin in place. Return legs to tucked position, if untucked. Place turkey, breast side up, on flat rack in shallow roasting pan. Brush with oil.

3. Roast turkey 1½ hours. Then, cover breast and top of drumsticks loosely with aluminum foil to prevent overcooking.

4. Continue roasting turkey 45 minutes to 1 hour. Uncover turkey breast and brush with honey-spice mixture. Cover breast with foil and continue roasting turkey 30 minutes to 1 hour* or until meat thermometer reaches 180°F when inserted into deepest part of thigh not touching bone.

5. Transfer turkey to cutting board; loosely tent with foil. Let stand 15 minutes before carving.

Follow cooking times according to package directions; times vary with size of turkey.

Makes 12 to 14 servings

Note: To grill turkey, prepare and cook turkey according to package directions, brushing occasionally with honey-spice mixture during the last 45 minutes of grilling.

---

tip

Roast Turkey for the new cook: *If you prefer, you can prepare your turkey without using the glaze. Just coat the turkey with oil as directed, and roast 1½ hours. After covering the breast and drumsticks with foil, continue roasting the turkey 1½ to 2 hours or until the meat thermometer reaches 180°F when inserted into deepest part of the thigh not touching bone.*

Orange Chile Marinated Roast Turkey

PREP 10 minutes   **MARINATE** 8 to 12 hours   **COOK** 3 to 3½ hours

ORANGE CHILE MARINADE

- 3 ancho chile peppers
- 1 head garlic
- 2 cups orange juice
- 3 cinnamon sticks
- 2 tablespoons cider vinegar
- 2 tablespoons crushed whole allspice berries
- 2 tablespoons crushed black peppercorns
- 1½ tablespoons kosher salt
- 6 bay leaves
- 1 teaspoon whole cloves
- 2 quarts ice-cold water

TURKEY

- 1 (12- to 14-pound) BUTTERBALL® Fresh or Frozen Whole Turkey, thawed if frozen
- Nonstick cooking spray

1. Remove stems from chiles; shake out seeds. Place in small saucepan and cover with water; bring to a boil over medium-high heat. Reduce heat; simmer 10 to 15 minutes or until chiles are soft. Transfer chiles to food processor or blender with slotted spoon; process until smooth, adding enough cooking water for even consistency. Set aside.

2. Cut garlic in half widthwise; remove as much peel as possible. Place in large stainless steel saucepan. Add orange juice, cinnamon, vinegar, allspice, pepper, salt, bay leaves and cloves; mix well. Bring to a boil over medium heat. Reduce heat to medium-low; simmer, uncovered, 10 minutes, stirring occasionally. Remove from heat. Pour into large nonmetallic container; stir in ice water and puréed chiles until evenly combined.

3. Remove neck and giblets from body and neck cavities of turkey. Refrigerate for another use or discard. Pat turkey dry with paper towels. Place turkey, breast side down, in marinade. Cover; refrigerate 8 to 12 hours, turning turkey over occasionally.

4. Preheat oven to 325°F. Remove turkey from marinade; discard marinade. Pat turkey dry with paper towels. Turn wings back to hold neck skin against back of turkey. Return legs to tucked position, if untucked. Place turkey, breast side up, on flat rack in shallow roasting pan; coat with cooking spray.

5. Roast turkey 1½ hours. Then, cover breast and top of drumsticks loosely with aluminum foil to prevent overcooking.

6. Continue roasting turkey 1½ to 2 hours* or until meat thermometer reaches 180°F when inserted into deepest part of thigh not touching bone.

7. Transfer turkey to cutting board; loosely tent with foil. Let stand 15 minutes before carving.

*Follow cooking times according to package directions; times vary with size of turkey.

Makes 10 to 12 servings

Maple-Basted Roast Turkey with Cranberry Pan Gravy

PREP 15 minutes   **COOK** 3½ to 4 hours

TURKEY

1 (12- to 16-pound) BUTTERBALL® Fresh or Frozen Whole Turkey, thawed if frozen

8 fresh sage leaves

¼ cup fresh lemon juice

⅔ cup pure maple syrup

CRANBERRY PAN GRAVY

Pan drippings

2½ cups chicken broth, divided

2 cups cranberry juice cocktail

2 tablespoons cornstarch

¾ cup sweetened dried cranberries

1. Preheat oven to 325°F. Remove neck and giblets from body and neck cavities of turkey. Refrigerate for another use or discard. Pat turkey dry with paper towels. Turn wings back to hold neck skin in place. Return legs to tucked position, if untucked. Place turkey, breast side up, on flat rack in shallow roasting pan. Gently loosen skin over breast; tuck sage leaves under skin. Brush turkey with lemon juice.

2. Roast turkey 1½ hours. Then, cover breast and top of drumsticks loosely with aluminum foil to prevent overcooking.

3. Continue roasting turkey 1 hour. Uncover turkey and baste every 15 minutes with maple syrup during last 30 minutes of roasting. Continue roasting turkey 30 minutes to 1 hour* or until meat thermometer reaches 180°F when inserted into deepest part of thigh not touching bone.

4. Transfer turkey to cutting board; loosely tent with foil. Let stand 15 minutes while preparing gravy.

5. Place roasting pan with drippings on burners over medium heat. Stir in ½ cup broth; bring to a boil, scraping browned bits from bottom of pan. Remove roasting pan from heat; strain mixture through fine-mesh sieve into large saucepan.

6. Add 1½ cups broth and cranberry juice cocktail. Bring to a boil over medium heat, stirring frequently; reduce heat to medium-low. Combine remaining ½ cup broth and cornstarch in small bowl; mix smooth. Stir cornstarch mixture into saucepan; add dried cranberries. Cook and stir 5 minutes or until gravy thickens. Serve with turkey.

Follow cooking times according to package directions; times vary with size of turkey.

Makes 10 to 14 servings

Marinated Grecian Roast Turkey

PREP 15 minutes   **MARINATE** 8 to 12 hours   **COOK** 3 to 3½ hours

GRECIAN MARINADE

- 1 **cup fresh lemon juice**
- 6 **stalks celery, chopped**
- ¼ **cup dried oregano**
- ¼ **cup olive oil**
- 2 **tablespoons kosher salt**
- 1 **tablespoon minced dried garlic**
- 1 **tablespoon onion powder**
- 2½ **cups water**

TURKEY

- 1 **(12- to 14-pound) BUTTERBALL® Fresh or Frozen Whole Turkey, thawed if frozen**
- **Grecian Rub (recipe follows)**
- **Vegetable oil**

1. Place lemon juice, celery, oregano, olive oil, salt, garlic and onion powder in food processor or blender. Process until evenly combined. Pour into large nonmetallic container; stir in water until well blended.

2. Remove neck and giblets from body and neck cavities of turkey. Refrigerate for another use or discard. Pat turkey dry with paper towels. Place turkey, breast side down, in marinade. Cover; refrigerate 6 to 8 hours, turning turkey over occasionally.

3. Prepare Grecian Rub. Remove turkey from marinade; discard marinade. Pat turkey dry with paper towels. Turn wings back to hold neck skin against back of turkey. Return legs to tucked position, if untucked. Place turkey, breast side up, on flat rack in shallow roasting pan. Brush breast and legs lightly with vegetable oil. Apply Grecian Rub on turkey skin; refrigerate 2 to 4 hours.

4. Preheat oven to 325°F. Roast turkey 1½ hours. Then, cover breast and top of drumsticks loosely with aluminum foil to prevent overcooking.

5. Continue roasting turkey 1½ to 2 hours* or until meat thermometer reaches 180°F when inserted into deepest part of thigh not touching bone.

6. Transfer turkey to cutting board; loosely tent with foil. Let stand 15 minutes before carving.

Follow cooking times according to package directions; times vary with size of turkey.

Makes 10 to 12 servings

Grecian Rub

¼ **cup lemon-pepper seasoning**

1½ **tablespoons dried oregano**

1 **tablespoon kosher salt**

1 **teaspoon black pepper**

Combine seasoning, oregano, salt and pepper in small bowl; mix well.

tip

The Grecian Rub mixture can be stored in an airtight container in a cool dry place for up to 3 weeks.

Floridian Citrus Brined Roast Turkey

PREP 30 minutes   **MARINATE** 12 hours   **COOK** 3 to 3½ hours

CITRUS BRINE

 1 **cup coarsely chopped onions**

 ½ **cup chopped fresh ginger**

 ⅓ **cup chopped garlic**

 3 **oranges, cut into quarters**

 2 **lemons, cut into quarters**

 1 **lime, cut into quarters**

 3 **tablespoons crushed
    black peppercorns**

10 **sprigs fresh thyme**

 6 **fresh bay leaves**

 1 **quart water**

 1 **cup kosher salt**

 ½ **cup firmly packed
    brown sugar**

 ½ **cup honey**

 1 **gallon ice-cold water**

TURKEY

 1 **(12- to 14-pound)
    BUTTERBALL® Fresh
    or Frozen Whole Turkey,
    thawed if frozen**

    Nonstick cooking spray

1. Place onions, ginger, garlic, oranges, lemons, lime, pepper, thyme and bay leaves in food processor or blender. Pulse 1 minute or until evenly combined. Pour mixture into large nonmetallic container or brining bag.

2. Heat 1 quart water in large saucepan; bring to a boil. Remove from heat. Add salt, brown sugar and honey; stir until dissolved. Cool mixture 30 minutes. Pour into container with citrus-spice mixture; stir in ice water.

3. Remove neck and giblets from body and neck cavities of turkey. Refrigerate for another use or discard. Pat turkey dry with paper towels. Place turkey, breast side down, in brine mixture. Cover; refrigerate 12 hours, turning turkey over occasionally.

4. Preheat oven to 325°F. Remove turkey from brine; discard brine. Pat turkey dry with paper towels. Turn wings back to hold neck skin against back of turkey. Return legs to tucked position, if untucked. Place turkey, breast side up, on flat rack in shallow roasting pan; coat with cooking spray.

5. Roast turkey 1½ hours. Then, cover breast and top of drumsticks loosely with aluminum foil to prevent overcooking.

6. Continue roasting turkey 1½ to 2 hours* or until meat thermometer reaches 180°F when inserted into deepest part of thigh not touching bone.

7. Transfer turkey to cutting board; loosely tent with foil. Let stand 15 minutes before carving.

Follow cooking times according to package directions; times vary with size of turkey.

Makes 10 to 12 servings

Roast Turkey with Mole Rub

PREP 10 minutes   **CHILL** 2 to 4 hours   **COOK** 3 to 3½ hours

MOLE RUB

- 2 **tablespoons ancho chile powder**
- 1 **tablespoon finely chopped salted peanuts**
- 1 **tablespoon toasted sesame seeds**
- 1 **tablespoon packed dark brown sugar**
- 2 **teaspoons chipotle chile powder**
- 2 **teaspoons unsweetened cocoa powder**
- 1½ **teaspoons kosher salt**
- 1½ **teaspoons black pepper**
- 1 **teaspoon roasted ground cumin**
- 1 **teaspoon minced dried garlic**
- ¼ **teaspoon anise seeds**
- ⅛ **teaspoon ground cloves**

TURKEY

- 1 **(12- to 14-pound) BUTTERBALL® Fresh or Frozen Whole Turkey, thawed if frozen**
- **Vegetable oil**

1. Combine ancho chile powder, peanuts, sesame seeds, brown sugar, chipotle chile powder, cocoa, salt, pepper, cumin, garlic, anise seeds and cloves in small bowl; mix well.

2. Remove neck and giblets from body and neck cavities of turkey. Refrigerate for another use or discard. Pat turkey dry with paper towels. Turn wings back to hold neck skin in place. Return legs to tucked position, if untucked. Place turkey, breast side up, on flat rack in shallow roasting pan. Brush breast and legs lightly with oil. Apply prepared rub on turkey skin; refrigerate 2 to 4 hours.

3. Preheat oven to 325°F. Roast turkey 1½ hours. Then, cover breast and top of drumsticks loosely with aluminum foil to prevent overcooking.

4. Continue roasting turkey 1½ to 2 hours* or until meat thermometer reaches 180°F when inserted into deepest part of thigh not touching bone.

5. Transfer turkey to cutting board; loosely tent with foil. Let stand 15 minutes before carving.

Follow cooking times according to package directions; times vary with size of turkey.

Makes 10 to 12 servings

tip

The Mole Rub mixture can be stored in an airtight container in a cool dry place for up to 3 weeks.

Roast Turkey with Beer Mop Basting Sauce

PREP 15 minutes   **CHILL** 1 to 2 hours   **COOK** 3 to 3½ hours

BEER MOP BASTING SAUCE

- 1 **can (12 ounces) beer**
- ½ **cup (1 stick) melted butter or vegetable oil**
- ½ **cup diced onion**
- 2 **canned chipotle peppers in adobo sauce,* chopped**
- 3 **tablespoons canned adobo sauce***
- 3 **tablespoons Worcestershire sauce**
- 2 **tablespoons smoked paprika**
- 2 **tablespoons chopped garlic**
- 1½ **teaspoons ancho chile powder**
- 1½ **teaspoons black pepper**
- 1 **teaspoon kosher salt**

TURKEY

- 1 **(12- to 14-pound) BUTTERBALL® Fresh or Frozen Whole Turkey, thawed if frozen**
- **Nonstick cooking spray**

*Canned chipotle peppers and adobo sauce can be found in the Mexican section of most supermarkets.

1. Pour beer into small stainless steel saucepan; bring to a boil over high heat. Reduce heat to medium-low; simmer, uncovered, 10 to 15 minutes or until reduced to ½ cup. Remove from heat.

2. Stir in butter, onion, chipotle peppers, adobo sauce, Worcestershire sauce, paprika, garlic, chile powder, black pepper and salt. Place mixture in food processor or blender; process until smooth. Transfer to covered container; refrigerate at least 1 to 2 hours.

3. Preheat oven to 325°F. Remove neck and giblets from body and neck cavities of turkey. Refrigerate for another use or discard. Pat turkey dry with paper towels. Turn wings back to hold neck skin in place. Return legs to tucked position, if untucked. Place turkey, breast side up, on flat rack in shallow roasting pan; coat with cooking spray.

4. Roast turkey 2 hours. Then, brush evenly with basting sauce. Cover breast and top of drumsticks loosely with aluminum foil to prevent overcooking. Continue roasting turkey 30 minutes. Uncover, brush with additional basting sauce, and return foil to cover breast and top of drumsticks.

5. Continue roasting turkey, basting occasionally, 30 minutes to 1 hour** or until meat thermometer reaches 180°F when inserted into deepest part of thigh not touching bone.

6. Transfer turkey to cutting board; loosely tent with foil. Let stand 15 minutes before carving.

**Follow cooking times according to package directions; times vary with size of turkey.

Makes 10 to 12 servings

Java Coffee-Rubbed Roast Turkey

PREP 10 minutes   **CHILL** 2 to 4 hours   **COOK** 3 to 3½ hours

JAVA COFFEE RUB

- ⅓ **cup firmly packed dark brown sugar**
- ⅓ **cup medium-fine grind dark-roasted coffee**
- 3 **tablespoons ancho chile powder**
- 2 **tablespoons kosher salt**
- 1 **tablespoon black pepper**
- 1 **tablespoon unsweetened cocoa**
- 2 **teaspoons minced dried garlic**
- 2 **teaspoons smoked paprika**
- ½ **teaspoon ground cumin**
- ½ **teaspoon dry mustard**

TURKEY

- 1 **(12- to 14-pound) BUTTERBALL® Fresh or Frozen Whole Turkey, thawed if frozen**
- **Vegetable oil**

1. Combine brown sugar, coffee, chile powder, salt, pepper, cocoa, garlic, paprika, cumin and mustard in small bowl; mix well.

2. Remove neck and giblets from body and neck cavities of turkey. Refrigerate for another use or discard. Pat turkey dry with paper towels. Turn wings back to hold neck skin in place. Return legs to tucked position, if untucked. Place turkey, breast side up, on flat rack in shallow roasting pan. Brush breast and legs lightly with oil. Apply prepared rub on turkey skin; refrigerate 2 to 4 hours.

3. Preheat oven to 325°F. Roast turkey 1½ hours. Then, cover breast and top of drumsticks loosely with aluminum foil to prevent overcooking.

4. Continue roasting turkey 1½ to 2 hours* or until meat thermometer reaches 180°F when inserted into deepest part of thigh not touching bone.

5. Transfer turkey to cutting board; loosely tent with foil. Let stand 15 minutes before carving.

Follow cooking times according to package directions; times vary with size of turkey.

Makes 10 to 12 servings

tip

The Java Coffee Rub mixture can be stored in an airtight container in a cool dry place for up to 3 weeks.

Roast Turkey with Spicy Rub

PREP 10 minutes   **CHILL** 12 hours   **COOK** 3 to 3½ hours

SPICY RUB

- 3 tablespoons firmly packed light brown sugar
- 3 tablespoons kosher or sea salt
- 3 tablespoons chili powder
- 2 teaspoons black pepper
- 2 teaspoons roasted ground cumin
- 2 teaspoons garlic powder
- 2 teaspoons crushed red pepper flakes
- 1 teaspoon ground coriander

TURKEY

- 1 (14- to 16-pound) BUTTERBALL® Fresh or Frozen Whole Turkey, thawed if frozen
- 6 tablespoons canola oil, divided

1. Combine brown sugar, salt, chili powder, black pepper, cumin, garlic powder, red pepper flakes and coriander in small bowl; mix well.

2. Remove neck and giblets from body and neck cavities of turkey. Refrigerate for another use or discard. Pat turkey dry with paper towels. Turn wings back to hold neck skin against back of turkey. Return legs to the tucked position, if untucked. Place turkey, breast side up, on flat rack in shallow roasting pan. Brush with 3 tablespoons oil. Apply prepared rub on skin and inside cavity. Cover; refrigerate at least 12 hours or overnight.

3. Preheat oven to 325°F. Brush outside of turkey with remaining 3 tablespoons oil.

4. Roast turkey 1½ hours. Then, cover breast and top of drumsticks loosely with aluminum foil to prevent overcooking. Continue roasting turkey 1½ to 2 hours* or until meat thermometer reaches 180°F when inserted into deepest part of thigh not touching bone.

5. Transfer turkey to cutting board; loosely tent with foil. Let stand 15 minutes before carving.

Follow cooking times according to package directions; times vary with size of turkey.

Makes 12 to 14 servings

Roast Turkey with Mediterranean Rub

PREP 10 minutes   **COOK** 3 to 3½ hours

MEDITERRANEAN RUB

- 1 **cup chopped fresh parsley**
- ¼ **cup ground dry lemon peel**
- 4 **teaspoons sugar**
- 4 **teaspoons sea salt**
- 4 **teaspoons chopped fresh rosemary**
- 1 **tablespoon dried oregano**
- 2 **teaspoons black pepper**
- ½ **teaspoon crushed red pepper flakes**

TURKEY

- 1 **(14- to 16-pound) BUTTERBALL® Fresh or Frozen Whole Turkey, thawed if frozen**
- **Nonstick cooking spray**

1. Preheat oven to 325°F. Combine parsley, lemon peel, sugar, salt, rosemary, oregano, black pepper and red pepper flakes in medium bowl; mix well. Cover; set aside.

2. Remove neck and giblets from body and neck cavities of turkey. Refrigerate for another use or discard. Pat turkey dry with paper towels. Turn wings back to hold neck skin against back of turkey. Return legs to the tucked position, if untucked. Place turkey, breast side up, on flat rack in shallow roasting pan. Coat evenly with cooking spray.

3. Roast turkey 1½ hours. Then, cover breast and top of drumsticks loosely with aluminum foil to prevent overcooking. Continue roasting turkey 1½ to 2 hours* or until meat thermometer reaches 180°F when inserted into deepest part of thigh not touching bone.

4. Transfer turkey to cutting board. Loosely tent with foil. Let turkey stand 15 minutes before sprinkling rub over entire turkey and carving.**

Follow cooking times according to package directions; times vary with size of turkey.

**Or sprinkle on turkey slices after carving.

Makes 12 to 14 servings

*Gravy, stuffing, and potatoes
naturally go well with turkey.
Expand your menu with
some savory new alternatives*

served
on the *side*

Whipped Potatoes with Roasted Cauliflower

PREP 20 minutes   **COOK** 45 minutes

1 **large head cauliflower,
cleaned and cut into florets**

7 **tablespoons olive oil, divided**

3¾ **teaspoons sea salt, divided**

1 **tablespoon minced garlic**

¾ **teaspoon black pepper**

3½ **pounds Yukon Gold potatoes,
peeled and cut into quarters**

1½ **cups warm milk**

¼ **cup (½ stick) butter, softened**

1. Preheat oven to 400°F.

2. Place cauliflower in large bowl.
Toss with 3 tablespoons oil,
¾ teaspoon salt, garlic and pepper.
Transfer to 13×9-inch pan. Bake
40 to 45 minutes or until cauliflower

is golden brown, stirring halfway
through baking time. Remove from
oven; cover with aluminum foil to
keep warm.

3. Meanwhile, place potatoes
in large saucepan with enough
water to cover; stir in remaining
3 teaspoons salt. Bring to a boil over
medium-high heat. Reduce heat to
medium-low; simmer, uncovered,
15 to 20 minutes or until potatoes
are tender when pierced with fork.

4. Drain potatoes; place in large
bowl. Add remaining 4 tablespoons
oil, milk and butter. Mash to smooth
consistency. Fold in roasted
cauliflower.

Makes 12 servings

Oyster Stuffing

PREP 20 minutes   **BAKE** 1 hour

1½ **pounds French bread,
cut into 1-inch cubes**

¾ **cup (1½ sticks) butter**

1 **clove garlic, minced**

1½ **cups diced celery**

1½ **cups diced onions**

3 **fresh bay leaves, chopped**

2 **tablespoons fresh thyme**

1 **tablespoon Old Bay
Seasoning**

10 **fresh sage leaves, chopped**

1 **teaspoon salt**

1 **teaspoon black pepper**

4 **cups chicken broth**

3 **large eggs, beaten**

⅓ **cup chopped fresh
Italian parsley**

1½ **pints shucked oysters**

1. Preheat oven to 350°F. Butter 3-quart covered casserole dish. Place bread cubes in single layer on large baking sheet. Bake 8 to 10 minutes or until bread is golden brown, stirring once during baking. Cool on wire rack.

2. Melt ¾ cup butter in large skillet over medium heat. Add garlic; cook and stir 1 minute. Add celery, onions and bay leaves; cook and stir 6 to 8 minutes or until vegetables are soft. Add thyme, seasoning, sage, salt and pepper; cook and stir 1 minute.

3. Combine broth and eggs in medium bowl. Place toasted bread in large bowl; stir in parsley and cooked vegetable mixture. Add oysters and three-fourths of broth mixture; stir in gently. Stuffing should be moist but not wet; add remaining broth mixture as necessary. Spoon stuffing into prepared casserole dish.

4. Cover; bake 30 minutes. Remove cover; bake 20 to 30 minutes longer or until top of stuffing is golden brown and crisp; center of stuffing should reach 165°F.

Makes 12 servings

tip

The bread cubes can be toasted one day in advance. Store in resealable plastic food storage bag until needed.

Sautéed Green Beans with Crunchy Almonds

PREP 15 minutes   **CHILL** 1 hour   **COOK** 10 minutes

2 **pounds green beans, trimmed**

3 **tablespoons unsalted butter**

1 **tablespoon olive oil**

½ **cup toasted slivered almonds***

2 **tablespoons chopped fresh parsley**

*To toast, spread in single layer in heavy-bottomed skillet. Cook over medium heat 1 to 2 minutes, stirring frequently, until nuts are lightly browned. Remove from skillet immediately. Cool before using.

1. Place green beans in large saucepan with enough water to cover. Bring to a boil over medium-high heat. Reduce heat to medium-low; simmer, uncovered, 4 to 6 minutes or until beans reach desired tenderness.

2. Drain beans and immerse in ice water. Let stand 3 to 5 minutes or until completely chilled. Drain; pat dry with paper towels. Place in resealable plastic food storage bag. Refrigerate at least 1 hour.

3. Heat butter and oil in large skillet over medium heat until butter is melted. Add beans; cook and stir 4 to 6 minutes or until light golden brown. Stir in almonds and parsley. Heat through and serve warm.

Makes 8 servings

tip

Green beans can be boiled up one day in advance. Cool and refrigerate as directed in step 2, then proceed as directed when ready to serve.

Catalan-Style Brussels Sprouts

PREP 15 minutes   **COOK** 15 minutes

- 2 **pounds Brussels sprouts, trimmed**
- ¼ **cup olive oil, divided**
- 8 **ounces chorizo sausage, removed from casing, cut in half horizontally, then cut into ¼-inch thick slices**
- ½ **cup diced onion**
- 4 **cloves garlic, minced**

1. Bring large pot of salted water to a boil over medium-high heat. Add Brussels sprouts; return to a boil. Reduce heat to medium-low; simmer, uncovered, 5 to 7 minutes or until fork-tender. Drain and immerse in ice water. Let stand 5 to 10 minutes or until completely chilled. Drain; pat dry with paper towels. Set aside.

2. Heat 2 tablespoons oil in large skillet over medium heat. Add chorizo, onion and garlic; cook and stir 3 to 5 minutes or until chorizo is golden brown. Transfer to plate.

3. Return skillet to medium heat; heat remaining 2 tablespoons oil. Add Brussels sprouts; cook and stir 4 to 6 minutes or until golden brown. Stir in chorizo mixture. Heat through and serve warm.

Makes 12 servings

Fresh Cranberry Sauce with Port Wine

PREP 10 minutes   **COOK** 20 minutes   **CHILL** 2 to 3 hours

SPICE BUNDLE

- 1 piece cheesecloth, 10 inches square
- 18 whole allspice berries
- 1 3-inch cinnamon stick, broken in half
- 8 whole black peppercorns
- 6 whole cloves
- 4 to 5 inches food-safe string

CRANBERRY SAUCE

- 1 package (12 ounces) fresh whole cranberries
- 1 Honey Crisp apple, peeled and diced
- 1 cup firmly packed light brown sugar
- 1 cup fresh orange juice
- 2 tablespoons fresh lemon juice
- ⅓ cup port wine

1. Spread cheesecloth on work surface. Place allspice, cinnamon, peppercorns and cloves in center; bring up sides to form bundle. Tie tightly with string.

2. Combine cranberries, apple, brown sugar, orange juice, lemon juice and prepared spice bundle in large saucepan; stir well. Bring to a boil over medium-high heat. Reduce heat to medium-low; simmer, uncovered, 15 to 20 minutes or until cranberries begin to pop and mixture thickens slightly, stirring frequently.

3. Remove and discard spice bundle. Refrigerate cranberry sauce in covered container 2 to 3 hours or until well chilled.*

4. Before serving, gently stir wine into cranberry sauce.

Cranberry sauce can be prepared the day before and refrigerated overnight.

Makes 12 servings

Bread Stuffing

PREP 20 minutes   **BAKE** 1 hour

1½ pounds French bread, cut
      into 1-inch cubes

¾ cup (1½ sticks) butter

1 clove garlic, minced

1½ cups diced celery

1½ cups diced onions

3 fresh bay leaves, chopped

2 tablespoons fresh thyme

10 fresh sage leaves, chopped

1 teaspoon salt

1 teaspoon black pepper

4 cups chicken broth

3 large eggs, beaten

⅓ cup chopped fresh
      Italian parsley

1. Preheat oven to 350°F. Butter 3-quart covered casserole dish. Place bread cubes in single layer on large baking sheet. Bake 8 to 10 minutes or until bread is golden brown, stirring once during baking. Cool on wire rack.

2. Melt ¾ cup butter in large skillet over medium heat. Add garlic; cook and stir 1 minute. Add celery, onions and bay leaves; cook and stir 6 to 8 minutes or until vegetables are soft. Add thyme, sage, salt and pepper; cook and stir 1 minute.

3. Combine broth and eggs in medium bowl. Place toasted bread in large bowl; stir in parsley and cooked vegetable mixture. Add three-fourths of broth mixture; stir in gently. Stuffing should be moist but not wet; add remaining broth mixture as necessary. Spoon stuffing into prepared casserole dish.

4. Cover; bake 30 minutes. Remove cover; bake 20 to 30 minutes longer or until top of stuffing is golden brown and crisp; center of stuffing should reach 165°F.

Makes 12 servings

---

tip

The bread cubes can be toasted one day in advance. Store in resealable plastic food storage bag until needed.

Pomegranate Gravy

PREP 5 minutes   **COOK** 20 minutes

3 **cups chicken broth**

1 **cup pomegranate juice**

½ **cup pomegranate molasses**

¼ **cup defatted turkey pan drippings**

Harissa paste,* to taste

Salt, to taste

*Harissa, a spicy red-pepper paste used in many North African cuisines, is available in the ethnic food aisle of many supermarkets and in specialty stores.

1. Combine broth, juice, molasses and pan drippings in medium saucepan; stir well. Bring to a boil over medium heat. Reduce heat to medium-low; simmer, uncovered, 15 to 20 minutes or until slightly thickened.

2. Strain gravy through fine-mesh sieve, if desired. Add harissa and salt to taste (gravy should be spicy); cook and stir until heated through.

Makes 12 servings

tip

If you can't find harissa paste, you can make your own. Remove stems and seeds from 5 dried red chiles; soak chiles in hot water 1 hour or until soft. Use slotted spoon to transfer chiles to food processor. Toast 3 tablespoons ground coriander and 2 tablespoons ground cumin in small skillet over medium-high heat 2 minutes or just until fragrant; add to food processor. Add 3 cloves garlic and 1 tablespoon salt to food processor. Pulse to combine ingredients. Slowly add ¼ cup extra-virgin olive oil while processor is running; process until paste forms. Store in refrigerator in airtight container.

Turkey Pan Gravy

PREP 10 minutes   **COOK** 20 minutes

¼ **cup defatted turkey pan drippings**

½ **cup all-purpose flour**

½ **teaspoon poultry seasoning**

¼ **teaspoon salt**

¼ **teaspoon black pepper**

3¾ **cups chicken broth**

1. Place pan drippings in medium saucepan. Add flour, seasoning, salt and pepper; mix until smooth. Gradually whisk in broth until smooth.

2. Bring to a boil over medium heat, stirring occasionally. Reduce heat to medium-low; simmer 5 minutes, stirring frequently, until gravy has thickened.

Makes 12 servings

tip

For a different flavor, substitute dry white wine for part of the broth, if desired. You can also increase the amount of poultry seasoning, to taste.

Vegetable Couscous Stuffing

PREP 25 minutes   **COOK** 15 minutes

⅓ **cup olive oil**

1½ **tablespoons minced garlic**

1 **cup diced onions**

1 **teaspoon black pepper**

1 **teaspoon ground turmeric**

1 **teaspoon roasted ground cinnamon**

1 **teaspoon roasted ground cumin**

½ **teaspoon cayenne pepper**

7 **cups chicken broth, heated**

2 **cups uncooked couscous**

1½ **cups shredded carrots**

1½ **cups shredded zucchini**

1 **cup raisins**

½ **cup toasted slivered almonds***

¼ **cup thinly sliced green onions**

1½ **tablespoons chopped fresh mint**

*To toast almonds, spread in single layer in heavy-bottomed skillet. Cook over medium heat 1 to 2 minutes, stirring frequently, until nuts are lightly browned. Remove from skillet immediately. Cool before using.

1. Heat oil in large saucepan over medium-high heat. Add garlic; cook and stir 1 minute. Add onions; cook and stir 3 minutes. Stir in black pepper, turmeric, cinnamon, cumin, and cayenne pepper.

2. Add broth and couscous; stir well. Bring to a boil. Stir in carrots and zucchini. Cover pan; remove from heat. Let stand 6 to 8 minutes or until broth is absorbed.

3. Fluff mixture with fork. Stir in raisins, almonds, green onions and mint. Serve warm.

Makes 12 servings

Roasted Parsnips, Carrots and Red Onion

PREP 15 minutes   **BAKE** 25 minutes

- **4 cups carrots, cut into 2-inch pieces**
- **4 parsnips, cut into 2-inch pieces**
- **1½ cups thinly sliced red onion**
- **2 tablespoons balsamic vinegar**
- **4 teaspoons extra-virgin olive oil**
- **½ teaspoon salt**
- **¼ teaspoon black pepper**

1. Preheat oven to 425°F. Lightly coat baking sheet with nonstick cooking spray.

2. Combine carrots, parsnips, onion, vinegar, oil, salt and pepper in large bowl. Mix until vegetables are evenly coated. Place on prepared baking sheet.

3. Bake 25 minutes or until vegetables are tender, stirring occasionally.

Makes 8 servings

Wild and Brown Rice Pilaf with Fresh Thyme and Sage

PREP 15 minutes   **BAKE** 20 minutes

3	tablespoons olive oil
1	tablespoon minced garlic
1¼	cups diced onions
1¼	cups uncooked long-grain brown rice
¾	cup uncooked wild rice
4½	cups hot chicken broth
1	tablespoon chopped fresh sage
1	tablespoon chopped fresh thyme
1	teaspoon sea salt
½	teaspoon black pepper

1. Preheat oven to 350°F. Heat oil in large ovenproof saucepan over medium heat. Add garlic; cook and stir 15 seconds. Add onions; cook and stir 5 minutes or until onions are softened.

2. Add brown rice and wild rice; cook and stir 1 minute. Add broth, sage, thyme, salt and pepper; stir well. Bring to a boil over medium-high heat. Cover with lid, and place in oven.

3. Bake 20 minutes or until broth is absorbed. Remove from oven and let rest, covered, 2 minutes. Fluff with fork before serving.

Makes 10 servings

served on the *side*

Lemony Pan-Grilled Asparagus with Olive Oil

PREP 10 minutes   **COOK** 5 to 7 minutes

3 pounds fresh asparagus, trimmed

¼ cup olive oil

3 tablespoons lemon zest

Lemon peel strips (optional)

1. Heat lightly oiled stovetop grilling pan over medium-high heat 3 to 4 minutes or until hot.

2. Dry asparagus with paper towels. Working in batches, place on hot pan. Turn asparagus to ensure grill marks on all sides. Cook and turn until crisp-tender. (Time will vary depending on thickness of asparagus.) Keep cooked asparagus warm. Repeat with remaining asparagus.

3. Arrange on serving platter. Drizzle with oil and sprinkle with lemon zest. Garnish with lemon peel strips.

Makes 10 servings

Whipped Potatoes
with Shredded Savoy Cabbage

PREP 20 minutes **COOK** 25 minutes

2½ **pounds Yukon Gold potatoes,
peeled and cut into quarters**

1½ **tablespoons sea salt**

1 **pound shredded
savoy cabbage**

1 **cup buttermilk,* warmed**

6 **tablespoons butter, softened**

**If you don't have buttermilk, substitute
1 tablespoon vinegar or lemon juice plus
enough milk to equal 1 cup. Let stand
5 minutes.*

1. Place potatoes in large saucepan
with enough water to cover; stir in
salt. Bring to a boil over medium-
high heat. Reduce heat to medium-
low; simmer, uncovered, 15 to
20 minutes or until potatoes are
tender when pierced with fork.

2. Add cabbage; cook 2 minutes or
until tender.

3. Drain potatoes and cabbage;
place in large bowl. Mash to chunky
consistency. Add buttermilk and
butter; mash to smooth consistency.

Makes 8 servings

Asiago Whipped Potatoes with Turkey Bacon

PREP 10 minutes   **COOK** 15 minutes

2 **pounds red potatoes, peeled and cut in half**

1 **tablespoon olive oil**

1 **large leek, white part only, cut in half lengthwise and thinly sliced**

5 **ounces grated Asiago cheese**

2 **tablespoons butter, softened**

Salt, to taste

Black pepper, to taste

¾ **cup BUTTERBALL® Turkey Bacon, cut into ¼-inch pieces and cooked until crisp**

1. Place potatoes in large saucepan with enough water to cover. Bring to a boil over medium-high heat. Reduce heat to medium-low; simmer, uncovered, 10 to 15 minutes or until tender when pierced with fork.

2. Heat oil in small skillet over medium heat. Add leek; cook and stir 2 to 3 minutes or until tender but not brown. Set aside.

3. Drain potatoes, reserving cooking liquid. Add cheese, butter and leek to potatoes. Mash until fairly smooth, adding ½ to ¾ cup reserved cooking liquid if necessary for desired consistency. Season with salt and pepper. Fold in turkey bacon.

Makes 8 servings

Baked Acorn Squash
with Brown Sugar and Butter

PREP 15 minutes   **BAKE** 1 hour 5 minutes

⅓ **cup firmly packed
   brown sugar**

4 **teaspoons ground cinnamon**

4 **acorn squash (each about
   1½ pounds), cut in half
   lengthwise, seeds removed**

½ **cup (1 stick) butter**

1. Preheat oven to 375°F. Combine brown sugar and cinnamon in small bowl; set aside.

2. Trim thin slice off side or bottom of each squash half so squash will stay upright when served. Place squash halves, cavity side down, on two rimmed baking pans.

3. Bake 50 to 60 minutes or until knife can easily be inserted. Remove from oven. Turn over; pierce bottoms with fork. Sprinkle cavities evenly with cinnamon mixture. Place 1 tablespoon butter in each squash. Return to oven 3 to 5 minutes or until butter is melted. Serve warm.

Makes 8 servings

You won't want to wait until midnight to raid the refrigerator when these delicious dishes are so easy to make any time of day

love those
leftovers

Turkey Pomodoro

PREP 30 minutes **COOK** 10 minutes

SAUCE

- ⅓ **cup olive oil**
- 3 **tablespoons minced garlic**
- 8 **cups diced plum tomatoes with juice**
- 1 **cup chopped fresh Italian parsley**
- 1 **cup pitted chopped kalamata olives**
- ⅓ **cup chopped fresh basil leaves**
- 3 **bay leaves**
- 2 **teaspoons dried oregano**
- 2 **teaspoons sugar**

PASTA

- 1¼ **pounds (6 cups) rigatoni pasta, cooked and drained**
- 2 **pounds leftover cooked BUTTERBALL® Turkey, cut into ¼-inch strips**

- 6 **tablespoons grated Parmesan cheese**
- 6 **tablespoons chopped fresh Italian parsley**

1. Heat oil in large saucepan over medium heat. Add garlic; cook and stir 30 seconds. Add tomatoes, 1 cup parsley, olives, basil, bay leaves, oregano and sugar; stir well. Bring to a boil. Reduce heat and simmer, uncovered, 5 minutes.

2. Add turkey to pasta sauce. Return to a boil and heat through. Remove bay leaves before serving.

3. Place pasta in large serving bowl. Top with pasta sauce, cheese and 6 tablespoons parsley.

Makes 6 servings

Savory Turkey Chili

PREP 20 minutes   **COOK** 30 minutes

2 tablespoons canola oil

2 teaspoons minced garlic

1 cup diced onions

2 tablespoons seeded diced
   jalapeño pepper*

2 teaspoons chili powder

2 teaspoons roasted
   ground cumin

2½ cups chopped
   leftover cooked
   BUTTERBALL® Turkey

2 cans (15 ounces each) red
   kidney beans, rinsed and
   drained

2 cups chicken broth

1 can (4 ounces) chopped mild
   green chiles, drained

¼ cup chopped fresh cilantro

6 tablespoons sour cream

6 tablespoons shredded
   Cheddar cheese or
   Monterey Jack cheese

6 tablespoons sliced
   green onions

   Oyster crackers (optional)

*Jalapeño peppers can sting and irritate
the skin, so wear rubber gloves when
handling peppers and do not touch your
eyes.

1. Heat oil in large saucepan over medium heat. Add garlic; cook and stir 30 seconds. Add onions; cook and stir 3 minutes.

2. Remove from heat. Stir in jalapeño pepper, chili powder and cumin. Return to heat. Stir in turkey, beans, broth, chiles and cilantro; bring to a boil. Reduce heat and simmer, uncovered, 25 minutes.

3. To serve, divide chili evenly among six bowls. Top each serving with 1 tablespoon sour cream, 1 tablespoon cheese and 1 tablespoon green onion. Serve with crackers, if desired.

Makes 6 servings

Turkey and Jasmine Rice Stuffed Peppers

PREP 30 minutes   **BAKE** 1½ hours

2 tablespoons olive oil

1 tablespoon minced garlic

2 cups diced onions

½ cup diced carrots

1½ pounds diced leftover cooked BUTTERBALL® Turkey

2¾ cups chicken broth, divided

2 cups cooked jasmine rice

1 cup grated Parmesan cheese

1 cup chopped fresh Italian parsley

¾ cup dry unseasoned bread crumbs

3 eggs, beaten

1 tablespoon chopped fresh sage

1 tablespoon chopped fresh thyme

4 red or green bell peppers, cut in half and seeds removed

4 cups Italian tomato sauce

2 bay leaves

1. Preheat oven to 325°F. Heat oil in medium skillet over medium heat. Add garlic; cook and stir 30 seconds. Add onions and carrots; cook and stir 3 minutes. Spoon mixture into large bowl.

2. Add turkey, ¾ cup broth, rice, cheese, parsley, bread crumbs, eggs, sage and thyme; mix well. Divide evenly among bell pepper halves. Place filled bell peppers in large baking pan.

3. Blend tomato sauce and remaining 2 cups broth. Stir in bay leaves. Spoon sauce evenly over and around bell peppers.

4. Bake 1¼ to 1½ hours or until bell peppers are tender. Remove bay leaves before serving.

Makes 4 servings

Bourbon Street BBQ Sliced Turkey

PREP 15 minutes **COOK** 15 minutes

SAUCE

- 1 cup sliced green onions
- 6 tablespoons Worcestershire sauce
- ⅓ cup minced garlic
- 2 tablespoons chili powder
- 2 tablespoons chopped fresh rosemary
- 2 tablespoons chopped fresh thyme
- 1 tablespoon black pepper
- 2 teaspoons dried oregano
- 1½ teaspoons cayenne pepper
- 1½ teaspoons crushed red pepper flakes
- 1½ teaspoons sea salt
- 2¼ cups dark beer
- 1 cup whipping cream
- ¾ cup (1½ sticks) butter, softened
- ¾ cup chopped fresh cilantro
- ½ cup chopped fresh chives

TURKEY

- 4½ cups hot cooked rice
- 1½ pounds sliced leftover cooked BUTTERBALL® Turkey, heated

1. Combine green onions, Worcestershire sauce, garlic, chili powder, rosemary, thyme, black pepper, oregano, cayenne pepper, red pepper flakes and salt in medium saucepan; mix well. Add beer; mix well. Cover; bring to a boil over medium heat. Reduce heat to medium-low; simmer, uncovered, until reduced by one-fourth.

2. Add cream; mix well. Remove from heat; add butter and stir until melted. Stir in cilantro and chives. Keep warm.

3. Divide rice among serving plates; top with turkey slices. Spoon sauce over turkey.

Makes 6 servings

Note: This sauce is also very good on grilled smoked turkey and turkey sausage.

Wild Rice and Turkey Soup

PREP 20 minutes   **COOK** 20 minutes

1 **tablespoon vegetable oil**

1 **cup finely chopped carrots**

1 **cup finely chopped onions**

½ **cup finely chopped celery**

2 **cloves garlic, minced**

2 **cups chopped leftover cooked BUTTERBALL® Turkey**

2 **cups cooked wild rice**

2 **cans (about 14 ounces each) chicken broth**

¼ **teaspoon salt**

¼ **teaspoon black pepper**

2 **cups whipping cream**

2 **tablespoons dry sherry**

1. Heat oil in large saucepan over medium-high heat. Add carrots, onions, celery and garlic. Cook and stir 5 minutes or until vegetables are tender.

2. Stir in turkey, rice, broth, salt and pepper. Cook 10 minutes, stirring occasionally.

3. Stir in cream and sherry. Cook until heated through, stirring occasionally. Serve immediately.

Makes 8 servings

Turkey Migas

PREP 20 minutes   **COOK** 15 minutes

10 **large eggs**

1 **teaspoon chili powder**

¼ **cup (½ stick) butter**

1 **cup onion, cut into 1½×¼-inch strips**

1 **cup seeded green bell pepper, cut into 1½×¼-inch strips**

1 **cup seeded red bell pepper, cut into 1½×¼-inch strips**

2 **cups diced leftover cooked BUTTERBALL® Turkey**

1 **cup (4 ounces) shredded pepper jack cheese**

4 **ounces corn chips**

20 **fresh cilantro leaves**

1 **cup prepared chunky salsa**

1. Beat eggs with chili powder in medium bowl; set aside.

2. Melt butter in large skillet over medium-high heat. Add onion and bell peppers; cook and stir 2 to 3 minutes or until crisp-tender.

3. Add turkey and egg mixture; stir well. Reduce heat to medium. When eggs begin to set, draw heatproof spatula along bottom and sides of skillet to loosen eggs. Stir in cheese. Continue to loosen cooked eggs from bottom and sides of skillet. Gently fold in corn chips. Continue cooking until egg mixture is set.

4. Spoon onto serving platter. Sprinkle with cilantro; pour salsa down center. Serve immediately.

Makes 6 servings

Turkey and Mushroom Stroganoff

PREP 15 minutes   **COOK** 25 minutes

5 **tablespoons butter, divided**

2 **teaspoons minced garlic**

2 **cups diced onions**

3 **cups sliced mushrooms**

½ **teaspoon black pepper**

¾ **cup dry white wine**

3 **cups prepared brown sauce***

2 **pounds shredded leftover cooked BUTTERBALL® Turkey**

2 **cups sour cream**

⅓ **cup chopped fresh dill**

8 **ounces (4 cups) uncooked egg noodles**

*Use purchased gravy from supermarket or gourmet shop, or prepare from dry mix.

1. Melt 3 tablespoons butter in large saucepan over medium heat. Add garlic; cook and stir 30 seconds. Add onions; cook and stir 8 minutes. Add mushrooms and pepper; cook and stir 3 to 5 minutes or until mushrooms are light golden brown. Add white wine; bring to a boil. Reduce heat to medium-low; simmer, uncovered, 10 minutes or until reduced by half.

2. Stir in brown sauce; bring to a boil. Reduce heat and simmer, uncovered, 3 minutes. Stir in turkey; heat through. Remove from heat; stir in sour cream and dill.

3. Meanwhile, cook noodles according to package directions; drain. Toss with remaining 2 tablespoons butter. Place on serving plate. Top with stroganoff mixture.

Makes 6 servings

Thai-Style Sliced Turkey with Coconut Curry Sauce

PREP 15 minutes **COOK** 35 minutes

COCONUT CURRY SAUCE

- **3 cups coconut milk**
- **2 tablespoons firmly packed brown sugar**
- **2 tablespoons fish sauce**
- **2 tablespoons Thai yellow curry paste**
- **1 tablespoon peeled minced fresh ginger**
- **1 jalapeño pepper,* seeded and diced**

TURKEY

- **2 tablespoons canola oil**
- **1 green bell pepper, seeded and cut into 2×¼-inch strips**
- **1 red bell pepper, seeded and cut into 2×¼-inch strips**
- **4½ cups hot cooked rice**
- **1½ pounds sliced leftover cooked BUTTERBALL® Turkey, heated**

*Jalapeño peppers can sting and irritate the skin, so wear rubber gloves when handling peppers and do not touch your eyes.

1. Combine coconut milk, brown sugar, fish sauce, curry paste, ginger and jalapeño pepper in medium saucepan; mix well. Bring to a boil over medium heat. Reduce heat to medium-low; simmer, uncovered, 15 minutes, stirring occasionally. Remove from heat; cool 30 minutes.

2. Pour cooled sauce into food processor; process until smooth. Return sauce to saucepan; heat to serving temperature.

3. Heat oil in large skillet over medium-high heat. Add bell peppers; cook and stir 4 to 6 minutes or until edges are golden brown and bell peppers are crisp-tender.

4. Place rice in center of serving plate; top with turkey slices. Spoon bell peppers around edge. Serve with sauce over all.

Makes 6 servings

tip

The sauce can be prepared in advance. After processing, store it in a covered container in the refrigerator. Bring to a boil before serving.

Turkey French Dip Panini

PREP 15 minutes   **COOK** 5 minutes

1 (6-inch) French bread roll, cut in half horizontally

2 teaspoons olive oil

1 tablespoon Dijon-style mayonnaise

1 tablespoon olive-oil mayonnaise

¼ cup sliced sautéed onions

4 ounces thinly sliced leftover cooked BUTTERBALL® Turkey

2 slices Asiago cheese

⅓ cup turkey gravy, heated

1. Brush outside top and bottom crusts of roll with olive oil.

2. Spread cut side of roll bottom with Dijon-style mayonnaise; spread cut side of roll top with olive-oil mayonnaise.

3. Place onions on roll bottom; top with turkey and cheese. Cover with roll top.

4. Grill in heated panini grill 4 to 6 minutes or until golden brown on both sides and cheese is melted. Cut sandwich in half; serve with gravy for dipping.

Makes 1 serving

tip

If you don't have a panini grill, coat a large heavy skillet or stovetop grill pan with nonstick cooking spray; heat over medium-low heat. Add the assembled panini. Weigh it down with a heatproof platter (if necessary, add a can or other weight to press down). Cook over low heat 3 to 4 minutes. Remove platter using oven mitt and turn over panini. Press down again; cook 3 minutes or just until cheese melts.

Open-Face Turkey Caprese Sandwich

PREP 15 minutes

1 **large diagonally sliced piece French bread, toasted**

1 **tablespoon olive-oil mayonnaise**

1 **to 2 small lettuce leaves**

4 **ounces thinly sliced leftover cooked BUTTERBALL® Turkey**

2 **slices tomato**

2 **slices fresh mozzarella cheese**

1 **teaspoon balsamic vinegar**

1 **teaspoon olive oil**

3 **fresh basil leaves, torn**

1. Spread one side of bread with mayonnaise. Top with lettuce, turkey, tomato slices and cheese.

2. Drizzle with vinegar and oil. Sprinkle with basil.

Makes 1 serving

Thai Turkey Wrap

PREP 15 minutes

3 tablespoons mayonnaise

¾ teaspoon prepared garlic chili sauce

1 (10-inch) flour tortilla

⅓ cup shredded lettuce

3 tablespoons shredded carrot

2 tablespoons thinly sliced green onion

¾ cup leftover cooked BUTTERBALL® Turkey, cut into 1×¼-inch strips

2 tablespoons prepared spicy peanut sauce

   Additional prepared spicy peanut sauce (optional)

1. Combine mayonnaise and chili sauce in small bowl. Heat tortilla in skillet or microwave about 10 seconds.

2. Spread one side of tortilla with mayonnaise mixture. Place lettuce down center; top with carrot, green onion, turkey and 2 tablespoons peanut sauce.

3. Fold bottom half of tortilla over filling; fold sides toward center, leaving top open. Serve with additional peanut sauce, if desired.

Makes 1 serving

tip

To make this wrap for a lunch box, fold it to enclose the filling completely: fold in two sides, then roll the tortilla up tightly from the bottom.

Turkey, Brie and Cranberry Apple Panini

PREP 10 minutes   **COOK** 5 minutes

2 slices multigrain bread

4 teaspoons butter, softened

2 tablespoons cranberry chutney or cranberry relish

1 tablespoon Dijon-style mayonnaise

3 ounces thinly sliced leftover cooked BUTTERBALL® Turkey

2 ounces sliced Brie cheese

3 thin slices unpeeled crisp apple, cored

4 spinach leaves, stems removed

1. Spread one side of each slice of bread with butter.

2. Spread other side of one slice with cranberry chutney; spread other side of second slice with mayonnaise.

3. Place turkey on chutney. Top with cheese slices, apple slices and spinach. Cover with second slice of bread, mayonnaise side down.

4. Grill in heated panini grill 4 to 6 minutes or until golden brown on both sides and cheese is melted. Cut sandwich in half and serve.

Makes 1 serving

tip

If you don't have a panini grill, coat a large heavy skillet or stovetop grill pan with nonstick cooking spray; heat over medium-low heat. Add the assembled panini. Weigh it down with a heatproof platter (if necessary, add a can or other weight to press down). Cook over low heat 3 to 4 minutes. Remove platter using oven mitt and turn over panini. Press down again; cook 3 minutes or just until cheese melts.

El Paso Turkey Quiche with Mango Cranberry Tomato Salsa

PREP 25 minutes   **CHILL** 2 hours   **BAKE** 45 minutes

MANGO CRANBERRY SALSA

- 2 ripe mangoes, peeled, seeded and diced
- 8 plum tomatoes, diced
- 1 cup diced green onions, white and green parts
- ⅔ cup chopped fresh cilantro
- ½ cup sweetened dried cranberries
- ½ cup fresh lime juice
- 4 cloves garlic, minced
- 1 jalapeño pepper,* seeded and thinly sliced
- 4 teaspoons chili powder
- 1 teaspoon hot sauce

QUICHE

- 1 refrigerated prepared pie crust (½ of 15-ounce package)
- 1 tablespoon butter
- ¼ cup diced onion
- 1 jalapeño pepper,* seeded and diced
- 1 teaspoon minced garlic
- 1 cup (4 ounces) shredded Monterey Jack cheese
- 6 large eggs, beaten
- 1 cup whole milk or half-and-half
- ½ teaspoon sea salt
- ¼ teaspoon black pepper
- 2 cups chopped leftover cooked BUTTERBALL® Turkey

*Jalapeño peppers can sting and irritate the skin, so wear rubber gloves when handling peppers and do not touch your eyes.

1. Combine mangoes, tomatoes, green onions, cilantro, cranberries, lime juice, 4 cloves garlic, sliced jalapeño pepper, chili powder and hot sauce in medium bowl. Refrigerate, covered, at least 2 hours.

2. Preheat oven to 425°F. Roll out pie dough on lightly floured surface to 11-inch circle. Press dough onto bottom and up sides of 9-inch deep-dish pie plate. Trim edges; flute if desired. (Do not prick dough.) Bake 10 to 12 minutes or until crust is light golden brown. Remove from oven.

3. Reduce oven temperature to 375°F. Melt butter in medium skillet over medium heat. Add onion, diced jalapeño pepper and 1 teaspoon garlic; cook and stir 3 to 4 minutes or until light golden brown. Transfer to plate; spread evenly and cover with plastic wrap. Place in freezer 10 minutes or until completely cooled.

4. Spread cheese evenly on bottom of parbaked pie crust. Sprinkle with cooled onion mixture and turkey. Whisk eggs, milk, ½ teaspoon salt and black pepper in medium bowl until well blended. Pour into parbaked pie crust.

5. Bake 30 to 40 minutes or until knife inserted near center comes out clean. Cool 10 minutes on wire rack. Serve with salsa.

Makes 6 servings

> ### *tip*
>
> *For a spicier flavor, use 2 jalapeño peppers in the quiche.*

Barley Turkey Vegetable Salad

PREP 25 minutes   **COOK** 10 minutes

2 cups water

½ teaspoon lemon pepper

**1 cup uncooked
    quick pearl barley**

**2 cups chopped
    leftover cooked
    BUTTERBALL® Turkey**

**½ pound cooked fresh
    asparagus spears, cut into
    1-inch pieces**

1 cup shredded red cabbage

**1 medium carrot, coarsely
    shredded**

¼ cup sliced green onions

2 tablespoons olive oil

2 tablespoons lemon juice

**1 tablespoon Dijon-style
    mustard**

1 teaspoon sugar

¼ teaspoon salt

1. Combine water and lemon pepper in medium saucepan; bring to a boil over medium-high heat. Stir in barley. Cover; reduce heat and simmer 10 minutes or until barley is tender. Remove from heat. Let stand, covered, 5 minutes. Drain if necessary. Place barley in large bowl; cool 10 minutes.

2. Add turkey, asparagus, cabbage, carrot and green onions; mix lightly.

3. Whisk oil, lemon juice, mustard, sugar and salt in small bowl until well blended. Pour dressing over barley mixture; mix lightly. Serve at room temperature.

Makes 6 servings

Turkey, Cheddar and Vegetable Frittata

PREP 10 minutes   **COOK** 2 minutes   **BAKE** 8 minutes

12 **large eggs**

1½ **cups diced leftover cooked BUTTERBALL® Turkey**

1 **cup diced leftover cooked vegetables**

1 **cup (4 ounces) shredded Cheddar cheese**

3 **tablespoons olive oil**

¼ **cup shredded or grated Parmesan cheese**

1. Preheat oven to 350°F. Beat eggs in large bowl. Stir in turkey, vegetables and Cheddar cheese.

2. Heat oil in 12-inch ovenproof skillet over medium-high heat. Pour in egg mixture. Cook 2 to 3 minutes or until eggs start to set around edges of skillet.

3. Place in oven. Bake 8 to 10 minutes or until top is firm and sides begin to pull away from edges.

4. Remove skillet from oven. Invert frittata onto serving platter. Before serving, sprinkle with Parmesan cheese.

Makes 8 servings

tip

Try this frittata with peas, corn, broccoli, asparagus, green beans or Brussels sprouts.

Turkey and Spinach Artichoke Dip

PREP 20 minutes   **BAKE** 30 minutes

2 **bags (6 ounces each) fresh baby spinach**

3 **tablespoons olive oil**

1 **cup diced onions**

1½ **teaspoons minced garlic**

2 **packages (8 ounces each) cream cheese, softened**

1 **cup ranch dressing**

1 **tablespoon hot sauce**

2 **cups diced leftover cooked BUTTERBALL® Turkey**

1 **can (about 14 ounces) artichoke hearts, drained and chopped**

1½ **cups (6 ounces) shredded Monterey Jack cheese**

½ **cup grated Parmesan cheese**

1 **cup (4 ounces) shredded Cheddar cheese**

Tortilla chips

1. Preheat oven to 325°F. Generously coat 1½-quart casserole dish or 9-inch square baking dish with nonstick cooking spray.

2. Bring large saucepan of water to a boil. Add spinach; cook 30 seconds or just until wilted. Drain; rinse under cold water. Squeeze out excess moisture. Chop; set aside.

3. Heat oil in medium skillet over medium heat. Add onions and garlic; cook and stir 3 to 5 minutes or until onions are soft. Remove from heat; cool.

4. Combine cream cheese, ranch dressing and hot sauce in large bowl; mix well. Stir in turkey, artichoke hearts, Monterey Jack cheese, Parmesan cheese, chopped spinach and cooled onion mixture. Spoon into prepared baking dish.

5. Bake 25 minutes. Remove from oven; sprinkle evenly with Cheddar cheese. Return to oven; bake 5 minutes or until cheese is completely melted. Serve warm with tortilla chips.

Makes 10 servings

Tex-Mex Turkey Rice Skillet

PREP 10 minutes   **COOK** 20 minutes

2 **tablespoons vegetable oil, divided**

1 **cup uncooked long-grain rice**

1 **can (about 14 ounces) chicken broth**

1 **cup medium or hot chunky salsa**

2 **cups chopped zucchini**

½ **cup chopped onion**

1 **cup frozen corn**

1½ **cups chopped leftover cooked BUTTERBALL® Turkey**

1 **cup (4 ounces) shredded Mexican-style cheese**

1. Heat 1 tablespoon oil in large skillet over medium heat. Add rice; cook and stir about 3 minutes or until rice turns light golden brown. Stir in broth and salsa. Cover; reduce heat to low and simmer 15 minutes or until rice is tender.

2. Meanwhile, heat remaining 1 tablespoon oil in another skillet over medium-high heat. Add zucchini and onion; cook and stir 3 minutes. Add corn; cook and stir 2 minutes or until vegetables just start to brown on edges. Stir in turkey; cover and keep warm until rice is done.

3. Add turkey mixture to cooked rice; cook 2 minutes or until heated through, stirring occasionally. Sprinkle evenly with cheese; cover. Remove from heat; let stand 5 minutes or until cheese is melted.

Makes 4 servings

Mediterranean Turkey Pasta Salad

PREP 30 minutes

1½ cups olive oil

½ cup red wine vinegar

1 tablespoon minced garlic

2 teaspoons dried oregano

3 cups diced leftover cooked BUTTERBALL® Turkey

3 cups cooked penne pasta

1 jar (16 ounces) pitted kalamata olives, drained and chopped

1 container (10 ounces) grape tomatoes, cut in half

8 ounces crumbled feta cheese

1 package (6 ounces) spring salad mix

½ cup chopped fresh Italian parsley

½ cup thinly sliced red onion

1. Whisk oil, vinegar, garlic and oregano in small bowl until well blended.

2. Combine turkey, pasta, olives, tomatoes, cheese, salad greens, parsley and red onion in large salad bowl. Gently toss with dressing. Refrigerate or serve at room temperature.

Makes 6 servings

For lunch, a quick bite, or meals on the go, you'll enjoy tasty favorites that take advantage of the convenience of turkey

lighter *fare*

Artisan Salad with Toasted Walnuts in Balsamic Vinaigrette

PREP 15 minutes   **CHILL** 1 hour

BALSAMIC VINAIGRETTE

- ½ cup plus 1 tablespoon white balsamic vinegar
- 1 teaspoon minced garlic
- 6 tablespoons olive oil
- 24 fresh basil leaves, chopped

SALAD

- 3 packages (6 ounces each) mixed baby field greens (spring mix)
- 1½ cups sweetened dried cranberries
- 1½ cups toasted chopped walnuts*
- 12 slices (1 ounce each) soft goat cheese

*To toast walnuts, spread in single layer in heavy-bottomed skillet. Cook over medium heat 1 to 2 minutes, stirring frequently, until nuts are lightly browned. Remove from skillet immediately. Cool before using.

1. Combine vinegar and garlic in small stainless steel bowl. Gradually whisk in oil until well blended. Fold in basil. Refrigerate at least 1 hour.

2. Toss greens, cranberries and walnuts in large salad bowl. Refrigerate, covered, until ready to serve.

3. To serve, gently toss salad with vinaigrette. Top each serving with 1 slice goat cheese.

Makes 12 servings

Honey-Roasted Pear Salad with Champagne and Port Wine Vinaigrette

PREP 25 minutes   **BAKE** 1 hour   **CHILL** 1 hour

HONEY-ROASTED PEARS

1½ tablespoons unsalted butter, softened

5 ripe Anjou pears, peeled, stems removed, cut in half and cored

3 tablespoons plus 1 teaspoon honey

CHAMPAGNE AND PORT WINE VINAIGRETTE

½ cup champagne vinaigrette

½ cup port wine

12 ounces dried figs, stems removed and cut into quarters

4 teaspoons firmly packed brown sugar

3 tablespoons white balsamic vinegar

3 tablespoons balsamic vinegar

2 shallots, minced

2 teaspoons Dijon-style mustard

¾ teaspoon kosher salt

¾ teaspoon black pepper

½ cup peanut oil

¼ cup walnut oil

SALAD

18 cups field greens

1 cup crumbled Gorgonzola cheese

¾ cup chopped walnuts

1. Preheat oven to 375°F. Spread butter evenly in bottom of 13×9-inch baking pan. Place pears in pan, cut side down. Drizzle each pear with 1 teaspoon honey.

2. Bake 40 minutes. Baste pears with pan juices. Bake 15 to 20 minutes more or until pears are caramelized. Remove from oven, baste pears with pan juices and cool on wire rack to room temperature. Cut pears into ⅜-inch slices; set aside.

3. Combine champagne vinaigrette, port wine, figs and brown sugar in medium saucepan; mix well. Bring to a boil over medium heat. Remove from heat; cool in pan 30 minutes.

4. Pour cooled fig mixture into stainless steel bowl. Whisk in balsamic vinegars, shallots, mustard, salt and pepper. Gradually whisk in peanut oil and walnut oil until well blended.

5. Combine greens, pears, cheese and walnuts in large salad bowl. Gently toss with 1½ cups dressing.

Makes 10 servings

Note: Refrigerate remaining dressing for another use. It will keep up to 2 weeks in an airtight container. Whisk well before using.

Tzatziki Cucumber Dip with Crudités

PREP 15 minutes   **CHILL** 2 hours

TZATZIKI CUCUMBER DIP

- 1 **cup peeled diced English cucumber**
- 2 **cups plain Greek yogurt**
- **Zest of 1 lemon**
- 3 **tablespoons fresh lemon juice**
- 2½ **tablespoons minced fresh mint**
- 2 **tablespoons olive oil**
- 1 **tablespoon minced garlic**
- 2 **teaspoons sea salt**
- 1½ **teaspoons white wine vinegar**

CRUDITÉS

- **Baby carrots**
- **Grape tomatoes**
- **Green onions, trimmed**
- **Zucchini, cut into pieces**
- **Bell peppers, cut into pieces**

1. Wrap cucumber in clean dish towel. Twist towel to squeeze juice from cucumber; discard juice.

2. Combine cucumber with yogurt, lemon zest, lemon juice, mint, oil, garlic, salt and vinegar in medium bowl; mix well. Refrigerate, covered, at least 2 hours.

3. Place dip in serving bowl. Serve with vegetables.

Makes 10 servings

Soft Turkey Tacos

PREP 5 minutes   **COOK** 15 minutes

8 **(6-inch) corn tortillas***

1½ **teaspoons vegetable oil**

1 **package (16 ounces) BUTTERBALL® Fresh Ground Turkey**

1 **small onion, chopped**

1 **teaspoon dried oregano**

  Salt, to taste

  Black pepper, to taste

  Chopped tomatoes

  Shredded lettuce

  Salsa

  Refried beans (optional)

*Substitute 8 (10-inch) flour tortillas for corn tortillas, if desired.

1. Wrap tortillas in foil. Place in cold oven; heat to 350°F.

2. Heat oil in large skillet over medium heat. Add turkey and onion; cook and stir until turkey is no longer pink (165°F). Stir in oregano. Season with salt and pepper.

3. Remove tortillas from oven and fill with turkey mixture; top with tomatoes, lettuce and salsa. Serve with refried beans, if desired.

Makes 4 servings

Note: To warm tortillas in microwave oven, wrap loosely in damp paper towel. Microwave on HIGH 2 minutes or until hot.

Grilled Turkey Cuban Sandwiches

PREP 15 minutes **COOK** 2 hours

---

1 (3-pound) BUTTERBALL®
  Boneless Breast of Turkey
  Roast, thawed

2 cloves garlic, sliced

1 tablespoon canola oil

1 tablespoon ground cumin

2 teaspoons salt

1 teaspoon coarsely ground
  black pepper

2 loaves Cuban, French or
  Italian Bread, 15 inches long

¼ cup honey mustard

½ pound smoked ham

½ pound sliced Swiss cheese

12 sandwich-style dill pickle
   slices

1. Spray cold grill grid with nonstick cooking spray. Prepare grill for medium indirect heat.

2. Remove turkey from package. Dry with paper towels. Discard gravy packet or refrigerate for another use (use within 2 to 3 days). Lift string netting and shift position on roast for easier removal after cooking. Cut small slits, at least 1 inch apart, over entire surface of turkey. Insert 1 garlic slice into each slit. Brush turkey with oil.

3. Combine cumin, salt and pepper in small bowl. Sprinkle evenly over turkey.

4. Place turkey on grill grid over drip pan. Cover grill with lid. Grill 1¼ to 1¾ hours or until meat thermometer reaches 170°F when inserted into center of roast. Remove from grill. Cover with aluminum foil and let stand 10 minutes.

5. Remove string netting. Cut half of turkey into 6 (⅛-inch-thick) slices; set aside. Refrigerate unsliced turkey for another use.

6. Cut each bread loaf into 3 pieces; slice each piece in half. Spread 2 teaspoons mustard on bottom half of each piece. Top with turkey slice, ham, cheese and pickles. Cover each with top of bread. Press sandwiches to flatten. Tightly wrap individually in aluminum foil.

7. Place wrapped sandwiches on grill grid. Top each with heavy iron skillet or brick. Grill 3 to 5 minutes on each side or until heated through. Serve warm.

Makes 6 servings

Carolina Turkey Burger

PREP 10 minutes   **COOK** 20 minutes

4 **BUTTERBALL® Original Seasoned Frozen Turkey Burgers**

½ **cup prepared barbecue sauce**

8 **slices (½ ounce each) Cheddar cheese**

¼ **cup Dijon-style mayonnaise**

4 **hamburger buns, split, buttered and toasted**

1⅓ **cups prepared coleslaw**

1. Prepare turkey burgers according to package directions for broiling.

2. When burgers are heated, top each with 1 tablespoon barbecue sauce and 2 slices cheese. Broil 1 minute or until cheese is melted.

3. Spread 1 tablespoon mayonnaise on bottom half of each hamburger bun. Top each with 1 cheese-topped burger and ⅓ cup coleslaw. Cover each with top of bun.

Makes 4 servings

Serving Suggestion: For an easy change of pace, try cooking burgers on the grill according to package directions.

Veggie-Packed Turkey Burgers

PREP 10 minutes **COOK** 10 minutes

1 **package (16 ounces) BUTTERBALL® Fresh Ground Turkey**

½ **cup chopped onion**

½ **cup shredded zucchini**

½ **cup shredded carrots**

1 **teaspoon minced jalapeño pepper***

Salt, to taste

Black pepper, to taste

Whole wheat rolls or hamburger buns

Shredded lettuce

Tomato slices

*Jalapeño peppers can sting and irritate the skin, so wear rubber gloves when handling peppers and do not touch your eyes.

1. Coat grill grid with nonstick cooking spray. Prepare grill for direct cooking.

2. Combine turkey, onion, zucchini, carrots, jalapeño pepper, salt and black pepper in large bowl. Form 4 (½-inch-thick) patties.

3. Grill, covered, 4 to 5 minutes per side over medium-high heat or until no longer pink and center of burgers reaches 165°F as measured with meat thermometer. Serve on rolls topped with lettuce and tomato slices.

Makes 4 servings

Italian Turkey Sausage Stew

PREP 10 minutes   **COOK** 20 minutes

3 links BUTTERBALL® Fresh Hot Italian Turkey Sausage (about 9 ounces), casings removed

1 green bell pepper, chopped

2 cloves garlic, minced

1 can (about 15 ounces) no-salt-added navy beans, rinsed and drained

1 can (about 14 ounces) Italian-style stewed tomatoes

1 cup turkey or chicken broth

1 teaspoon dried rosemary

1. Cook and stir turkey sausage in large saucepan over medium-high heat 6 to 8 minutes or until no longer pink (165°F). Drain any fat.

2. Add bell pepper and garlic; cook and stir 1 minute or until garlic is fragrant. Add beans, tomatoes, broth and rosemary; bring to a simmer. Cover; simmer over medium-low heat 5 minutes or until bell pepper is tender.

Makes 4 servings

BLT Turkey Burger

PREP 10 minutes   **COOK** 20 minutes

¼ **cup mayonnaise**

1½ **teaspoons honey**

1 **teaspoon chipotle pepper sauce**

1 **teaspoon chopped fresh cilantro**

4 **BUTTERBALL® Original Seasoned Frozen Turkey Burgers**

4 **slices (½ ounce each) Cheddar jack cheese**

4 **Kaiser rolls, split and toasted**

1 **cup shredded lettuce**

1 **avocado, cut into 8 slices**

4 **slices BUTTERBALL® Turkey Bacon, cooked and cut in half**

4 **slices tomato**

4 **slices red onion (about ⅛-inch thick)**

1. Combine mayonnaise, honey, chipotle pepper sauce and cilantro in small bowl. Refrigerate until ready to use.

2. Prepare turkey burgers according to package directions for broiling.

3. When burgers are cooked, top each with 1 slice cheese. Broil 1 minute or until cheese is melted.

4. Spread 1½ teaspoons mayonnaise mixture on cut sides of each roll. Layer each bottom half with ¼ cup shredded lettuce and 2 slices avocado. Top each with cheese-topped burger, 2 turkey bacon pieces, tomato and red onion. Cover each with top of roll.

Makes 4 servings

Franks Hawaiian-Style

PREP 10 minutes   **COOK** 10 minutes

6 slices fresh or canned
   pineapple, drained

2 teaspoons vegetable oil

1 cup mango salsa

1 tablespoon chopped
   fresh cilantro

2 teaspoons pickled ginger

1 package (16 ounces)
   BUTTERBALL® Bun Size
   Premium Turkey Franks

8 hot dog buns, split and
   toasted

3 tablespoons Dijon-style
   mustard

6 slices BUTTERBALL®
   Turkey Bacon, cooked
   and crumbled

1. Prepare grill for direct grilling over medium heat. Lightly brush pineapple with oil. Grill 1 to 2 minutes per side or until golden brown. Cut into 1/4-inch pieces; place in medium bowl. Stir in salsa, cilantro and ginger. Refrigerate until ready to use.

2. Grill franks, turning frequently, 6 to 10 minutes or until heated through. Serve in buns with mustard and pineapple mixture; sprinkle evenly with turkey bacon.

Makes 8 servings

Spicy Thai Sausage Salad

PREP 20 minutes   **COOK** 10 minutes

THAI RED CURRY VINAIGRETTE

- ½ **cup prepared Asian sesame dressing**
- 3 **tablespoons fresh lime juice**
- 2 **teaspoons dark sesame oil**
- 1 **teaspoon Thai red curry paste***

SALAD

- 1 **package (14 ounces) BUTTERBALL® Smoked Turkey Dinner Sausage, cut in half lengthwise, then diagonally cut into ¼-inch slices**
- 4 **cups torn Romaine lettuce**
- 2 **cups shredded iceberg lettuce**
- ½ **cup torn fresh basil leaves**
- 2 **cups thinly sliced seedless cucumber**
- 1 **cup red onion, cut into 2-inch strips**
- 1 **cup shredded carrots**
- ½ **cup chopped roasted peanuts**

*Thai red curry paste can be found in the Asian section of most supermarkets.

1. Combine sesame dressing, lime juice, sesame oil and red curry paste in small bowl; mix well. Refrigerate until ready to serve.

2. Heat turkey sausage in microwave according to package directions, reducing heating time to 3 to 4 minutes or until heated through. Drain on paper towels.

3. Toss Romaine lettuce, iceberg lettuce and basil in large bowl. Divide evenly among serving plates. Arrange warmed sausage over lettuce mixture. Sprinkle with cucumbers, red onion, carrots and peanuts. Drizzle with vinaigrette.

Makes 4 servings

Asian Lettuce Wraps

PREP 10 minutes

2 cups shredded cabbage or coleslaw mix

2 cups cut-up raw vegetables, such as carrots, red or green bell peppers, green onions, water chestnuts or bean sprouts

6 ounces BUTTERBALL® Deli Oven Roasted Turkey Breast, diced

⅓ cup dry-roasted unsalted peanuts

⅓ cup stir-fry sauce

1 to 2 tablespoons honey

12 whole Bibb or Boston lettuce leaves

Whole fresh chives (optional)

1. Combine shredded cabbage, vegetables, turkey and peanuts in medium bowl. Add stir-fry sauce and honey. Toss gently and thoroughly to coat completely.

2. Fill each leaf with about ½ cup cabbage mixture.

3. Fold up bottom and two sides to form wraps. Tie closed with whole chives, if desired.

Makes 4 servings

tip

For nuttier flavor, toast peanuts in a nonstick skillet over medium-high heat 3 minutes or until fragrant and beginning to brown. Immediately remove from skillet.

Turkey Club Salad

PREP 10 minutes

8 large romaine lettuce leaves

¼ pound sliced BUTTERBALL® Oven Roasted Turkey Breast

2 medium tomatoes, cut into 8 slices each

2 tablespoons BUTTERBALL® Turkey Bacon, cooked, drained and diced

¼ cup fat-free ranch salad dressing

Black pepper (optional)

Layer lettuce, turkey slices, tomato slices and turkey bacon on two plates. Drizzle with dressing or serve dressing on the side. Season with pepper, if desired.

Makes 2 servings

Easy Three-Bean Turkey Chili

PREP 5 minutes   **COOK** 6 to 8 hours (HIGH)

1 package (16 ounces) BUTTERBALL® Fresh Ground Turkey

1 small onion, chopped

1 can (28 ounces) diced tomatoes, undrained

1 can (about 15 ounces) chickpeas, rinsed and drained

1 can (about 15 ounces) kidney beans, rinsed and drained

1 can (about 15 ounces) black beans, rinsed and drained

1 can (8 ounces) tomato sauce

1 can (4 ounces) diced mild green chiles

1 to 2 tablespoons chili powder

Shredded Cheddar cheese (optional)

SLOW COOKER DIRECTIONS

1. Cook and stir turkey and onion in medium skillet over medium-high heat until no longer pink (165°F). Drain any fat. Transfer to slow cooker.

2. Add remaining ingredients; mix well. Cover; cook on HIGH 6 to 8 hours.

3. Sprinkle with cheese before serving, if desired.

Makes 6 to 8 servings

Lunch Wraps

PREP 10 minutes

4 **teaspoons yellow or Dijon honey mustard**

2 **(8-inch) flour tortillas**

2 **slices American cheese, cut in half**

¼ **pound thinly sliced BUTTERBALL® Oven Roasted Turkey Breast**

½ **cup matchstick or shredded carrot (about 1 medium)**

3 **romaine lettuce leaves, torn into bite-size pieces**

1. Spread 2 teaspoons mustard evenly over each tortilla.

2. Top each tortilla with 2 cheese halves, half of turkey, half of shredded carrot and half of torn lettuce.

3. Roll up tortillas; cut in half.

Makes 2 servings

Toasted Cobb Salad Sandwiches

PREP 5 minutes   **COOK** 10 minutes

½ **medium avocado**

1 **green onion, chopped**

½ **teaspoon lemon juice**

   Salt, to taste

   Black pepper, to taste

2 **Kaiser rolls, split**

¼ **pound thinly sliced BUTTERBALL® Oven Roasted Turkey Breast**

4 **slices BUTTERBALL® Fully Cooked Turkey Bacon**

1 **hard-cooked egg, sliced**

2 **slices (1 ounce each) Cheddar cheese**

2 **ounces blue cheese**

   Tomato slices (optional)

   Olive oil

1. Mash avocado in small bowl; stir in green onion and lemon juice. Season with salt and pepper. Spread avocado mixture on cut side of top half of each Kaiser roll.

2. Layer turkey slices, turkey bacon, egg, Cheddar cheese, blue cheese and tomato, if desired, on bottom half of each roll. Cover each with top of roll. Brush outsides of sandwiches lightly with oil.

3. Heat large nonstick skillet over medium heat. Add sandwiches; cook 4 to 5 minutes per side or until cheese melts and sandwiches are golden brown.

Makes 2 sandwiches

Make each day a celebration of family and friends with flavorful entrées that are quick and easy to prepare

everyday *meals*

Spicy Turkey with Citrus au Jus

PREP 10 minutes   **COOK** 4 to 5 hours (LOW) or 2½ to 3 hours (HIGH)

1 **(4-pound) BUTTERBALL® Fresh or Frozen Whole Turkey Breast, thawed, if frozen, rinsed and patted dry**

¼ **cup (½ stick) butter, softened**

Zest of 1 lemon

1 **teaspoon chili powder**

¼ **to ½ teaspoon black pepper**

⅛ **to ¼ teaspoon red pepper flakes**

1 **tablespoon lemon juice**

SLOW COOKER DIRECTIONS

1. Lightly coat slow cooker with nonstick cooking spray. Remove and discard turkey skin. Place turkey breast in slow cooker.

2. Combine butter, lemon peel, chili powder, black pepper and red pepper flakes in small bowl; mix well. Spread over top and sides of turkey. Cover; cook on LOW 4 to 5 hours or on HIGH 2½ to 3 hours or until temperature registers 170°F on meat thermometer inserted into thickest part of breast not touching bone.

3. Transfer turkey to cutting board. Let stand 10 minutes before slicing.

4. Stir lemon juice into cooking liquid. Strain; discard solids. Let mixture stand 15 minutes. Skim and discard excess fat. Serve with turkey.

Makes 6 to 8 servings

Classic Smoked Sausage Mac and Cheese

PREP 5 minutes   **COOK** 15 minutes   **BAKE** 25 minutes

1 **pound cavatappi (corkscrew) pasta, cooked and drained**

1 **package (14 ounces) BUTTERBALL® Smoked Turkey Dinner Sausage, cut in half lengthwise, then cut diagonally into ¼-inch slices**

¼ **cup (½ stick) plus 1 tablespoon butter, melted, divided**

1 **cup chopped onions**

3 **cups prepared Alfredo sauce**

3 **cups half-and-half**

1½ **pounds pasteurized prepared cheese product, cut into cubes**

2 **cups (8 ounces) shredded sharp Cheddar cheese**

½ **teaspoon black pepper**

1 **cup panko bread crumbs**

1. Preheat oven to 375°F. Coat 13×9-inch baking dish with nonstick cooking spray.

2. Heat 1 tablespoon butter in large saucepan over medium heat. Add sausage and onions; cook and stir 3 to 5 minutes or until onions are tender. Stir in Alfredo sauce and half-and-half. Bring to a boil, stirring constantly. Reduce heat; simmer 1 minute.

3. Remove from heat. Add cheese cubes, shredded Cheddar cheese and pepper; stir until cheese is melted. Add pasta; mix well. Pour into prepared baking dish. Combine bread crumbs and remaining ¼ cup melted butter in small bowl. Sprinkle evenly over top of mixture.

4. Bake 20 to 25 minutes or until hot and bubbly and crumbs are golden brown.

Makes 10 servings

Serving suggestion: Serve with a green salad to round out the meal.

Slow Cooker Turkey Breast

PREP 5 minutes   **COOK** 6 to 8 hours (LOW)

1 (3-pound) BUTTERBALL®
   **Boneless Turkey Breast
   Roast, thawed, if frozen,
   rinsed and patted dry**

Garlic powder

Paprika

Dried parsley flakes

SLOW COOKER DIRECTIONS

1. Season turkey with garlic powder, paprika and parsley. Place turkey in slow cooker.

2. Cover; cook on LOW 6 to 8 hours or until center of roast reaches 170°F as measured with meat thermometer.

3. Transfer turkey to cutting board. Cover with foil; let stand 10 to 15 minutes before carving.

Makes 4 to 6 servings

Pastitsio

PREP 5 minutes   **COOK** 20 minutes   **BAKE** 40 minutes

8 ounces elbow macaroni, cooked and drained

2 eggs, lightly beaten, or ½ cup cholesterol-free egg substitute

¼ teaspoon ground nutmeg

1 package (16 ounces) BUTTERBALL® Fresh Ground Turkey

½ cup chopped onion

1 clove garlic, minced

1 can (8 ounces) tomato sauce

¾ teaspoon dried mint

½ teaspoon dried oregano

½ teaspoon black pepper

⅛ teaspoon ground cinnamon

2 teaspoons butter or margarine

3 tablespoons all-purpose flour

1½ cups fat-free (skim) milk

2 tablespoons grated Parmesan cheese

1. Preheat oven to 350°F. Lightly coat 9-inch square baking dish with nonstick cooking spray.

2. Combine macaroni, eggs and nutmeg in prepared baking dish; mix well.

3. Cook and stir turkey, onion and garlic in large nonstick skillet over medium heat 6 to 8 minutes or until turkey is no longer pink (165°F). Stir in tomato sauce, mint, oregano, pepper and cinnamon. Reduce heat; simmer 10 minutes. Spread evenly over macaroni in baking dish.

4. Melt butter in small saucepan. Add flour; cook and stir 1 minute. Whisk in milk; cook 6 minutes or until thickened, stirring constantly. Pour sauce over meat mixture. Sprinkle with cheese.

5. Bake 30 to 40 minutes. Let stand 10 minutes before serving.

Makes 6 servings

Turkey Breast and Sweet Potatoes

PREP 30 minutes   **COOK** 2 hours

1 **tablespoon all-purpose flour**

1 **(6-pound) BUTTERBALL® Fresh or Frozen Whole Turkey Breast, thawed if frozen**

3 **large sweet potatoes, peeled and cut into 1-inch slices**

2 **medium Granny Smith apples, peeled and chopped**

1 **medium onion, sliced and separated into rings**

½ **cup frozen apple juice concentrate, thawed**

1 **teaspoon soy sauce**

1 **teaspoon dried thyme**

½ **teaspoon coarsely ground black pepper**

¼ **cup cold water**

2 **tablespoons cornstarch**

   Oven cooking bag

1. Preheat oven to 350°F. Add flour to large oven-cooking bag; close and shake to coat inside of bag. Place bag in 15×10-inch baking pan.

2. Remove gravy packet from turkey breast. Refrigerate for another use or discard. Pat turkey dry with paper towels; place in oven-cooking bag. Add potatoes, apples and onion.

3. Combine juice concentrate, soy sauce, thyme and pepper in small bowl; mix well. Pour over ingredients in bag. Close bag with tie; cut 6 (½-inch-long) slits in top of bag to vent.

4. Roast turkey breast 1½ to 1¾ hours* or until meat thermometer reaches 170°F when inserted into thickest part of breast. Remove from oven. Let stand 5 minutes.

5. Cut bag open carefully. Transfer turkey to cutting board; loosely tent with foil. Place sweet potatoes on serving platter; cover to keep warm. Pour juices from bag into 1-quart microwavable cup or bowl (there should be about 2 cups); discard bag. Stir water and cornstarch in small bowl until smooth; stir into juices. Microwave on HIGH 2½ minutes or until thickened, stirring in 1-minute intervals. Serve with turkey and sweet potatoes.

Follow cooking times according to package directions; times vary with size of turkey breast.

Makes 8 servings

Chili Wagon Wheel Casserole

PREP 5 minutes   **COOK** 15 minutes   **BAKE** 25 minutes

8 ounces wagon wheel or other pasta, cooked and drained

1 package (16 ounces) BUTTERBALL® Fresh Ground Turkey

¾ cup chopped onion

¾ cup chopped green bell pepper

1 can (about 14 ounces) no-salt-added stewed tomatoes

1 can (8 ounces) no-salt-added tomato sauce

½ teaspoon black pepper

¼ teaspoon ground allspice

½ cup (2 ounces) shredded Cheddar cheese

1. Preheat oven to 350°F.

2. Lightly coat large nonstick skillet with nonstick cooking spray; heat over medium-high heat. Add turkey; cook and stir 5 to 6 minutes until no longer pink (165°F). Add onion and bell pepper; cook and stir until tender.

3. Stir in tomatoes, tomato sauce, black pepper and allspice; cook 2 minutes. Stir in pasta. Spoon mixture into 2½-quart casserole. Sprinkle with cheese.

4. Bake 20 to 25 minutes or until heated through.

Makes 6 servings

Smoked Sausage with Mediterranean-Style Vegetables

PREP 10 minutes   **MARINATE** 30 minutes   **COOK** 10 to 20 minutes

2 **zucchini, sliced lengthwise into ½-inch slices, then cut in half**

6 **slices eggplant, ¾ inch thick**

2 **red onions, sliced ½ inch thick**

2 **tomatoes, sliced ½ inch thick**

½ **cup reduced-fat balsamic vinaigrette dressing**

1 **package (14 ounces) BUTTERBALL® Polska Kielbasa Turkey Dinner Sausage**

3 **ounces crumbled feta cheese**

6 **fresh basil leaves**

½ **cup reduced-fat red wine vinaigrette**

1. Place zucchini, eggplant, onions and tomatoes in resealable plastic food storage bag or glass dish. Add balsamic vinaigrette; seal bag and toss to coat vegetables evenly. Refrigerate 30 minutes to marinate.

2. Preheat grill to medium.

3. Remove vegetables from marinade. Grill sausage, zucchini, eggplant and onions 8 to 10 minutes, turning frequently until sausage is heated through and vegetables are tender. Add tomatoes during last 2 minutes of cooking, turning after 1 minute.

4. Cut sausage into diagonal slices. Divide sausage and vegetables evenly among serving plates. Top with cheese and basil leaves. Drizzle with red wine vinaigrette.

Makes 6 servings

Smoked Sausage Frittata

PREP 15 minutes   **COOK** 15 minutes   **BAKE** 5 minutes

1 package (14 ounces) BUTTERBALL® Smoked Turkey Dinner Sausage, cut in half lengthwise, then cut into ¼-inch slices

1½ tablespoons olive oil

1 cup diced green onions, white and green parts

10 large eggs, lightly beaten

¾ cup shredded mozzarella cheese

⅓ cup freshly grated Parmesan cheese

16 torn fresh basil leaves

¼ cup chopped sun-dried tomatoes

¼ teaspoon black pepper

Additional freshly grated Parmesan cheese (optional)

Additional fresh basil leaves (optional)

1. Preheat oven to 350°F.

2. Heat oil in heavy medium oven-proof skillet over medium heat. Add sausage and green onions; cook and stir 5 minutes or until light golden brown.

3. Combine eggs, mozzarella cheese, ⅓ cup Parmesan cheese, torn basil, tomatoes and pepper in medium bowl; mix well. Add to skillet. Cook over medium heat, lifting edges with rubber spatula to allow uncooked portion to flow underneath. Cook just until egg mixture begins to set, about 6 minutes.

4. Place skillet in oven. Bake 5 to 7 minutes or until egg mixture is firm to the touch and top is golden brown.

5. Remove skillet from oven. Carefully run spatula around edge to loosen frittata. Invert onto serving platter. Before serving, sprinkle with additional Parmesan cheese and garnish with basil leaves, if desired.

Makes 6 servings

Roast Turkey Breast with Sausage and Apple Stuffing

PREP 15 minutes   **COOK** 20 minutes   **BAKE** 1¾ hours

- **8 ounces bulk pork sausage**
- **1 medium apple, peeled and finely chopped**
- **1 shallot or small onion, finely chopped**
- **1 stalk celery, finely chopped**
- **¼ cup chopped hazelnuts**
- **½ teaspoon rubbed sage, divided**
- **½ teaspoon salt, divided**
- **½ teaspoon black pepper, divided**
- **1 tablespoon butter, softened**
- **1 (5½-pound) BUTTERBALL® Fresh or Frozen Whole Turkey Breast, thawed if frozen, rinsed and patted dry**
- **4 to 6 fresh sage leaves (optional)**
- **1 cup chicken or turkey broth**

1. Preheat oven to 325°F. Crumble sausage into large skillet. Add apple, shallot and celery; cook and stir over medium-high heat until sausage is no longer pink (165°F) and apple and vegetables are tender. Drain fat.

2. Stir in hazelnuts, ¼ teaspoon rubbed sage, ¼ teaspoon salt and ¼ teaspoon pepper. Spoon mixture into shallow roasting pan.

3. Combine butter and remaining rubbed sage, salt and pepper. Spread over turkey breast. Arrange fresh sage leaves under skin, if desired. Place flat rack on top of stuffing. Place turkey on rack. Pour broth into pan.

4. Roast 45 minutes. Baste with broth. Continue roasting turkey breast 1 hour* or until meat thermometer reaches 170°F when inserted into thickest part of breast not touching bone.

5. Remove from oven. Let stand 10 minutes before slicing.

Follow cooking times according to package directions; times vary with size of turkey breast.

Makes 6 servings

Apple-Brined Roasted Turkey Breast

PREP 10 minutes   **MARINATE** 6 to 8 hours   **BAKE** 2 hours

3 **quarts water**

2 **quarts apple juice**

1 **cup kosher salt**

3 **bay leaves**

2 **large cloves garlic, crushed**

1 **tablespoon crushed black peppercorns**

1 **(3-pound) BUTTERBALL® Boneless Turkey Breast Roast, thawed, rinsed and patted dry**

Ginger-Cranberry Chutney (recipe follows)

2 **tablespoons olive oil, divided**

1 **teaspoon salt**

½ **teaspoon black pepper**

½ **teaspoon smoked paprika or paprika**

1. Bring water, apple juice, kosher salt, bay leaves, garlic and peppercorns to a boil in Dutch oven or large saucepan, stirring until salt dissolves. Remove from heat; cool.

2. Lift string netting and shift position on turkey roast to make removal easier after roasting. Place turkey in brining container or bag. Pour cooled brine over turkey. Cover; refrigerate 6 to 8 hours, turning turkey occasionally.

3. Meanwhile, prepare Ginger-Cranberry Chutney.

4. Preheat oven to 325°F. Remove turkey from brine; discard brine. Rinse turkey briefly with cool water; drain and pat dry with paper towels. Rub with 1 tablespoon oil; sprinkle with 1 teaspoon salt and pepper.

5. Place turkey, skin side up, on flat rack in shallow roasting pan. Roast 1 hour. Combine remaining 1 tablespoon oil and paprika. Brush oil mixture onto turkey breast. If roast gets too brown, cover loosely with aluminum foil to prevent overcooking. Continue roasting turkey 45 minutes to 1 hour or until meat thermometer reaches 170°F when inserted into center of roast.

6. Remove from oven. Cover with foil and let stand 15 minutes before removing netting and carving. Serve with any natural juices and Ginger-Cranberry Chutney.

Makes 6 servings

Ginger-Cranberry Chutney

- **4 cups fresh or frozen cranberries**
- **1 cup sugar**
- **⅔ cup water**
- **½ cup dried cranberries**
- **2 tablespoons cider vinegar**
- **2 teaspoons grated fresh ginger**
- **1 teaspoon black pepper**
- **½ teaspoon salt**

Combine all ingredients in medium saucepan. Bring to a boil; reduce heat and simmer over medium heat 20 minutes or until cranberries burst and chutney thickens. Cool to room temperature. Chutney can be stored, covered, in refrigerator for up to 1 week.

Makes about 2 cups

Turkey Bacon, Potato and Cheddar Anytime Frittata

PREP 10 minutes   **COOK** 20 minutes

2 **teaspoons olive oil, divided**

½ **cup finely chopped green bell pepper**

½ **cup finely chopped red bell pepper**

½ **cup finely chopped onion**

1 **cup frozen shredded potatoes or hash brown potatoes, partially thawed**

2 **eggs, lightly beaten**

¼ **teaspoon salt**

⅛ **teaspoon black pepper**

⅛ **teaspoon dried thyme**

4 **slices BUTTERBALL® Turkey Bacon, cooked, drained and chopped**

2 **tablespoons finely shredded Cheddar cheese**

1. Heat 1 teaspoon oil in small nonstick skillet over medium-high heat. Add bell peppers and onion; cook and stir 3 to 4 minutes or until onion is translucent.

2. Reduce heat to medium-low. Sprinkle potatoes over vegetables in skillet. Drizzle remaining 1 teaspoon oil evenly over potatoes. Carefully pour in eggs; sprinkle evenly with salt, black pepper and thyme. Top evenly with turkey bacon. Cover and cook 10 minutes or until knife inserted near center comes out clean.

3. Remove from heat; sprinkle evenly with cheese. Cover and let stand 2 minutes or until cheese is melted. Cut into wedges.

Makes 2 servings

Note: A frittata is an Italian omelet in which the eggs are combined, before cooking, with other ingredients, such as meat, vegetables, and herbs. The egg mixture is poured into a heavy skillet and cooked slowly over low heat. This frittata can be served for breakfast, lunch, or dinner.

tip

Be sure to let the frittata stand a few minutes before serving to achieve the proper texture.

Four-Cheese Turkey Mac and Cheese

PREP 10 minutes   **COOK** 15 minutes   **BAKE** 25 minutes

2½ cups elbow macaroni,
     cooked and drained

2 cups chopped
   leftover cooked
   BUTTERBALL® Turkey

1 can (12 ounces) evaporated
   milk

3 eggs, slightly beaten

2 tablespoons Dijon-style
   mustard

2 teaspoons Worcestershire
   sauce

¼ teaspoon black pepper

2 cups (8 ounces) shredded
   Cheddar cheese

½ cup (2 ounces) shredded
   Swiss cheese

½ cup (2 ounces) shredded
   mozzarella cheese

½ cup grated or shredded
   Parmesan cheese

2 tablespoons butter, melted

¼ teaspoon garlic powder

1 cup fresh soft white or
   whole wheat bread crumbs

1. Preheat oven to 350°F. Coat 3-quart casserole dish with nonstick cooking spray.

2. Combine macaroni and turkey in large bowl. In separate large bowl, combine evaporated milk, eggs, mustard, Worcestershire sauce and pepper. Gradually stir cheeses into milk mixture. Stir milk mixture into pasta mixture.

3. Spoon into prepared casserole dish. Combine melted butter and garlic powder in small bowl. Stir in bread crumbs until evenly coated. Sprinkle bread crumb mixture over top of pasta.

4. Bake 25 to 30 minutes or until heated through and cheese is melted.

Makes 6 servings

Variation: Substitute provolone and Asiago cheeses for the Swiss and mozzarella.

Turkey Burgers with Creole Gravy

PREP 15 minutes   **COOK** 10 to 20 minutes

CREOLE GRAVY

- 3 tablespoons butter
- 1 tablespoon minced garlic
- 1 cup diced green bell peppers
- 1 cup diced onions
- ½ cup diced celery
- 1 can (about 14 ounces) fire-roasted diced tomatoes, undrained
- 1 jar (about 12 ounces) prepared turkey gravy
- 3 tablespoons Cajun seasoning
- 1 tablespoon Worcestershire sauce

TURKEY BURGERS

- 1 package (16 ounces) BUTTERBALL® Fresh All Natural Turkey Burger Patties
- 4 slices warm French bread, cut diagonally

1. Melt butter in 2-quart saucepan over medium-high heat. Add garlic; cook and stir 1 minute. Add bell peppers, onions and celery; cook and stir 5 minutes. Add tomatoes, gravy, Cajun seasoning and Worcestershire sauce. Bring to a boil. Reduce heat; simmer, uncovered, 15 minutes.

2. Coat medium skillet with nonstick cooking spray; heat over medium heat. Place patties in skillet; cook 4 to 5 minutes on each side, or until meat thermometer inserted in centers reaches 165°F.

3. Place 1 bread slice on each serving plate. Top with burger; serve with gravy.

Makes 4 servings

*Enjoy your seasonal favorites,
or try something new—either way,
be sure to save room for dessert!*

for your *sweet* tooth

Homemade Pumpkin Pie

PREP 20 minutes   **BAKE** 55 to 65 minutes

- 1   **refrigerated prepared pie crust (½ of 15-ounce package)**
- 2   **tablespoons pumpkin pie spice**
- 1   **tablespoon sugar**
- ½   **teaspoon salt**
- 3   **large eggs, beaten**
- 2½ **teaspoons vanilla**
- 1   **can (15 ounces) solid-pack pumpkin**
- ⅓   **cup sour cream**
- 1   **can (14 ounces) sweetened condensed milk (NOT evaporated milk)**
-     **Whipped cream (optional)**

1. Preheat oven to 425°F. Roll out pie dough on lightly floured surface to 11-inch circle. Press dough onto bottom and up sides of 9-inch deep-dish pie plate. Fold extra dough under and flute edges; set aside.

2. Combine pie spice, sugar and salt in large bowl. Whisk in eggs and vanilla until smooth. Add pumpkin and sour cream; mix until smooth. Gradually mix in sweetened condensed milk; mix until well blended. Pour into prepared crust.

3. Bake 15 minutes at 425°F. Reduce oven temperature to 350°F. Continue baking 40 to 45 minutes or until knife inserted near center comes out clean. Cool on wire rack at least 1½ hours before serving. Top each piece with whipped cream, if desired.

Makes 8 servings

tip

Prepare pie a day ahead of time; cool as directed, then refrigerate overnight. Remove 1 hour before serving. Preheat oven to 250°F; heat pie 15 minutes.

Pound Cake with Limoncello and Sweet Spiced Apples

PREP 10 minutes   **COOK** 5 minutes

Sweet Spiced Apples (recipe follows)

12 slices pound cake, cut ⅜ inch thick

¾ cup Limoncello

¾ cup whipped cream

¾ cup toasted chopped pecans*

To toast pecans, spread in single layer in heavy-bottomed skillet. Cook over medium heat 1 to 2 minutes, stirring frequently, until nuts are lightly browned. Remove from skillet immediately. Cool before using.

1. Prepare Sweet Spiced Apples. Keep warm.

2. To serve, toast pound cake slices; place on dessert plates. Top each with large spoonful of Sweet Spiced Apples, 1 tablespoon Limoncello, 1 tablespoon whipped cream and 1 tablespoon nuts.

Makes 12 servings

Sweet Spiced Apples

⅓ cup unsalted butter

⅓ cup firmly packed brown sugar

2 teaspoons ground cinnamon

¼ teaspoon ground nutmeg

⅛ teaspoon sea salt

⅛ teaspoon ground cloves

6 pounds Granny Smith apples, cored, peeled and sliced ¼ inch thick

1. Melt butter in large skillet over medium heat. Stir in brown sugar, cinnamon, nutmeg, salt and cloves; mix well. Add apples; toss carefully in butter mixture to prevent apples from breaking up. Cook 5 minutes or until apples are tender.

2. Hold warm until served.

Makes 12 servings

tip

Sweet Spiced Apples also make a tasty side dish for roast turkey or pork and are a delicious dessert for gluten-free diets when served alone or with whipped cream or ice cream.

Indian Pudding with Vanilla Ice Cream

PREP 15 minutes   **COOK** 25 minutes   **BAKE** 2½ to 3 hours

3 cups whole milk

⅓ cup yellow cornmeal

⅓ cup firmly packed
   dark brown sugar

⅓ cup light molasses

½ teaspoon salt

¼ cup (½ stick) butter

1 large egg, beaten

½ teaspoon ground cinnamon

½ teaspoon ground ginger

1 cup whipping cream

   Vanilla ice cream

1. Preheat oven to 275°F. Place milk in top of double boiler over simmering water; heat to a simmer. Gradually whisk in cornmeal; mix until smooth. Cook 15 minutes, stirring constantly.

2. Add brown sugar, molasses and salt; cook and stir 8 minutes.

3. Remove from heat. Add butter, egg, cinnamon and ginger; mix well. Pour into 1½-quart casserole. Pour cream over top. Cover casserole.

4. Bake 2½ to 3 hours, stirring every 30 minutes, until pudding is just set in center and still soft. Let stand 30 minutes to cool and thicken slightly. Serve warm with ice cream.

Makes 8 servings

tip

Light molasses can be hard to find. If your market doesn't have it, combine ⅔ cup dark molasses with ⅓ cup corn syrup to make the equivalent of 1 cup light molasses. Store the extra mixture in an airtight container for another use.

Mini Pumpkin Cheesecakes

PREP 20 minutes   **BAKE** 20 to 30 minutes

1 **cup ground walnuts**

½ **cup plus 4 teaspoons sugar, divided**

1 **tablespoon margarine or butter, melted**

2 **packages (8 ounces each) reduced-fat cream cheese, softened**

½ **cup canned pumpkin**

½ **teaspoon vanilla**

½ **teaspoon ground cinnamon**

Dash ground nutmeg

Dash ground cloves

2 **eggs**

Light whipped cream or whipped topping

Additional ground cinnamon (optional)

1. Preheat oven to 325°F.* Line 36 mini muffin pan cups with paper baking cups.

2. Combine walnuts, 4 teaspoons sugar and margarine in medium bowl; mix well. Press about 1 teaspoon firmly onto bottom of each prepared muffin cup. Bake 5 minutes; cool.

3. Beat cream cheese, pumpkin, remaining ½ cup sugar, vanilla, ½ teaspoon cinnamon, nutmeg and cloves in large bowl with electric mixer at medium speed until well blended. Add eggs, one at a time, beating at low speed after each addition until smooth. Divide evenly over prepared crusts.

4. Bake 15 minutes or until centers are almost set. Cool completely on wire racks; refrigerate at least 2 hours or until chilled. Top with whipped cream before serving; sprinkle with cinnamon, if desired.

*If using dark nonstick pans, preheat oven to 300°F.

Makes 18 servings

Pumpkin Pie in Gingersnap Pecan Crust

PREP 20 minutes   **BAKE** 55 to 65 minutes

CRUST

1¼ **cups gingersnap crumbs**

½ **cup all-purpose flour**

½ **cup chopped pecans**

⅓ **cup firmly packed
    light brown sugar**

1 **tablespoon crystallized
    ginger**

¼ **teaspoon salt**

⅓ **cup butter, melted**

FILLING

1 **tablespoon granulated sugar**

1 **tablespoon ground cinnamon**

2 **teaspoons ground ginger**

1 **teaspoon ground cloves**

1 **teaspoon ground nutmeg**

½ **teaspoon salt**

3 **large eggs, beaten**

2½ **teaspoons vanilla**

1 **can (15 ounces) solid-pack
    pumpkin**

⅓ **cup sour cream**

1 **can (14 ounces) sweetened
    condensed milk (NOT
    evaporated milk)**

   Whipped cream (optional)

1. Place gingersnap crumbs, flour, pecans, brown sugar, crystallized ginger and ¼ teaspoon salt in food processor. Process until finely chopped. Add melted butter; process until well blended.

2. Press onto bottom and up sides of 9-inch deep-dish pie plate; set aside.

3. Preheat oven to 425°F. Combine granulated sugar, cinnamon, ground ginger, cloves, nutmeg and ½ teaspoon salt in large bowl; mix well. Whisk in eggs and vanilla until smooth. Add pumpkin and sour cream; mix until smooth. Gradually mix in sweetened condensed milk; mix until well blended. Pour into prepared crust.

4. Bake 15 minutes at 425°F. Reduce oven temperature to 350°F. Continue baking 40 to 45 minutes or until knife inserted near center comes out clean. Cool on wire rack at least 1½ hours before serving. Top with whipped cream, if desired.

Makes 8 servings

---

tips

Prepare pie a day ahead of time; cool as directed, then refrigerate overnight. Remove 1 hour before serving. Preheat oven to 250°F; heat pie 15 minutes.

Use a paper stencil or doily to add a decorative touch. Just before serving, lay the stencil on the pie and dust with powdered sugar. Carefully remove the stencil.

Praline-Topped Apple Cranberry Bread Pudding

PREP 30 minutes   **SOAK** 8 to 12 hours   **BAKE** 40 to 50 minutes

4 **cups peeled and sliced Granny Smith apples (about 2 large apples)**

1 **cup sweetened dried cranberries**

½ **cup plus 2 tablespoons granulated sugar, divided**

1 **tablespoon ground cinnamon**

8 **large eggs**

2 **cups firmly packed light brown sugar, divided**

4 **cups half-and-half**

1 **tablespoon vanilla**

2 **teaspoons grated orange peel**

⅛ **teaspoon salt**

24 **slices (16 cups) Brioche or dense white bread, cut into 1-inch cubes and toasted**

⅓ **cup butter, softened**

1 **cup chopped pecans**

Butter Rum Sauce (optional, recipe follows)

1. Grease 13×9-inch baking dish. Combine apples, cranberries, 2 tablespoons granulated sugar and cinnamon in medium bowl; mix well. Set aside.

2. Combine eggs, remaining ½ cup granulated sugar and 1 cup brown sugar in separate medium bowl. Beat with mixer at high speed 3 minutes; reduce speed to low. Gradually mix in half-and-half, vanilla, orange peel and salt.

3. Place bread cubes in large bowl. Stir apple mixture into bread cubes, blending well. Pour beaten egg mixture over bread mixture; mix well.

4. Pour bread mixture evenly into prepared baking dish. Cover; refrigerate overnight.

5. Preheat oven to 350°F.

6. Combine butter, remaining 1 cup brown sugar and pecans in small bowl.

7. Remove bread pudding from refrigerator; uncover. Sprinkle nut mixture evenly over top.

8. Bake 40 to 50 minutes or until knife inserted near center comes out clean. Cool 20 minutes on wire rack before serving. Serve with Butter Rum Sauce, if desired.

Makes 18 servings

Butter Rum Sauce

- **1 cup (2 sticks) butter**
- **¾ cup granulated sugar**
- **¾ cup firmly packed light brown sugar**
- **⅓ cup powdered sugar**
- **2 egg yolks**
- **¼ cup whipping cream**
- **⅓ cup dark rum**

1. Whisk butter and all sugars in heavy saucepan until smooth. Cook over low heat, whisking frequently until small bubbles form around edge of mixture.

2. Whisk egg yolks and cream in small bowl until blended. Slowly whisk ½ cup hot butter mixture into egg yolk mixture. Pour mixture back into saucepan in slow stream, whisking constantly. Continue whisking over low heat 5 minutes or until mixture has thickened slightly. Do not boil.

3. Remove from heat; stir in rum. Serve warm.

Makes 18 servings

Southern Pecan Pie with Toffee Crunch

PREP 20 minutes   **BAKE** 40 to 45 minutes

1 **refrigerated prepared pie crust (½ of 15-ounce package)**

1¼ **cups dark corn syrup**

4 **eggs, lightly beaten**

¼ **cup (½ stick) butter, melted and cooled slightly**

2 **teaspoons vanilla**

1½ **cups pecan halves**

1 **cup toffee baking bits, divided**

1 **tablespoon all-purpose flour**

1. Preheat oven to 350°F. Roll pie crust into 12-inch circle on lightly floured work surface. Place in 9-inch pie pan; fold extra dough under and flute edge.

2. Combine corn syrup, eggs, butter and vanilla in medium bowl; mix well. Stir in pecans. Toss ⅔ cup baking bits with flour in small bowl; stir into pecan mixture. Pour into prepared pie shell.

3. Bake 40 to 45 minutes or until knife inserted in center comes out clean. Remove pie from oven; immediately sprinkle evenly with remaining baking bits. Cool completely on wire rack.

Makes 8 servings

Apple Cranberry Streusel Pie

PREP 30 minutes **BAKE** 1 hour

- 1 **refrigerated prepared pie crust (½ of 15-ounce package)**
- ¾ **cup all-purpose flour**
- ¾ **cup plus 6 tablespoons packed light brown sugar, divided**
- 6 **tablespoons uncooked old-fashioned oats**
- ½ **teaspoon ground cinnamon**
- 6 **tablespoons butter, melted**
- 2 **pounds Granny Smith apples, peeled and thinly sliced (5 cups)**
- 1 **can (about 16 ounces) whole-berry cranberry sauce**
- 1½ **tablespoons cornstarch**

1. Preheat oven to 350°F. Roll pie crust into 12-inch circle on lightly floured work surface. Place in 9-inch pie pan; fold extra dough under and flute edge.

2. Combine flour, 6 tablespoons brown sugar, oats and cinnamon in medium bowl; mix well. Stir in butter until mixture is crumbly; set aside.

3. Place apples and cranberry sauce in large bowl. Combine remaining ¾ cup brown sugar and cornstarch in small bowl; mix well. Sprinkle over apples; toss gently until apples are evenly coated. Transfer to prepared pie crust. Sprinkle evenly with oat mixture.

4. Bake 1 hour or until apples are tender. Transfer to wire rack to cool. Serve warm.

Makes 8 servings

Cake and Ice Cream "Pops"

PREP 25 minutes   **FREEZE** 45 to 50 minutes

- 1 **(10- to 12-ounce) pound cake**
- 1 **pint ice cream, any flavor**
- 1½ **bottles (7¼ ounces each) hard-coating chocolate topping**
- 10 **mini forks or wooden picks**
- **Multicolor sprinkles**
- **Finely chopped nuts**
- **Crushed chocolate sandwich cookies**
- **Chopped peppermint sticks**
- **Toasted coconut**

1. Line tray with plastic wrap. Remove pound cake from packaging. Slice ¼-inch thick piece from each end; reserve for another use. Cut remaining cake into ¾-inch thick slices. Cut circles with 1¾-inch diameter cookie cutter.

2. Place circles on prepared tray.

3. Top each cake circle with small scoop of ice cream, about 1¾-inch diameter.* Freeze 45 to 60 minutes or until ice cream is firm.

4. Pour chocolate topping into bowl. Remove prepared cake from freezer. Insert fork through ice cream into each piece of cake. Dip into chocolate topping to coat completely. Before coating dries, sprinkle with desired topping. Place pops on serving tray. Return to freezer 5 to 10 minutes or until coating is firm.

*A #20 ice cream scoop will make balls about 1¾ inches in diameter.

Makes 10 servings

tips

Coordinate the pops with any occasion. For example, use holiday flavors of ice cream such as pumpkin, cranberry or caramel to make the dessert festive throughout the fall and winter holidays, or decorate with seasonal candies for Valentine's Day or Easter.

Break leftover pieces of pound cake into small pieces and top with fresh fruit and whipped cream for a quick anytime dessert.

index

vegetables

metric conversion chart

VOLUME MEASUREMENTS (dry)

1/8 teaspoon = 0.5 mL
1/4 teaspoon = 1 mL
1/2 teaspoon = 2 mL
3/4 teaspoon = 4 mL
1 teaspoon = 5 mL
1 tablespoon = 15 mL
2 tablespoons = 30 mL
1/4 cup = 60 mL
1/3 cup = 75 mL
1/2 cup = 125 mL
2/3 cup = 150 mL
3/4 cup = 175 mL
1 cup = 250 mL
2 cups = 1 pint = 500 mL
3 cups = 750 mL
4 cups = 1 quart = 1 L

VOLUME MEASUREMENTS (fluid)

1 fluid ounce (2 tablespoons) = 30 mL
4 fluid ounces (1/2 cup) = 125 mL
8 fluid ounces (1 cup) = 250 mL
12 fluid ounces (1 1/2 cups) = 375 mL
16 fluid ounces (2 cups) = 500 mL

WEIGHTS (mass)

1/2 ounce = 15 g
1 ounce = 30 g
3 ounces = 90 g
4 ounces = 120 g
8 ounces = 225 g
10 ounces = 285 g
12 ounces = 360 g
16 ounces = 1 pound = 450 g

DIMENSIONS

1/16 inch = 2 mm
1/8 inch = 3 mm
1/4 inch = 6 mm
1/2 inch = 1.5 cm
3/4 inch = 2 cm
1 inch = 2.5 cm

OVEN TEMPERATURES

250°F = 120°C
275°F = 140°C
300°F = 150°C
325°F = 160°C
350°F = 180°C
375°F = 190°C
400°F = 200°C
425°F = 220°C
450°F = 230°C

BAKING PAN SIZES

Utensil	Size in Inches/Quarts	Metric Volume	Size in Centimeters
Baking or Cake Pan (square or rectangular)	8×8×2	2 L	20×20×5
	9×9×2	2.5 L	23×23×5
	12×8×2	3 L	30×20×5
	13×9×2	3.5 L	33×23×5
Loaf Pan	8×4×3	1.5 L	20×10×7
	9×5×3	2 L	23×13×7
Round Layer Cake Pan	8×1½	1.2 L	20×4
	9×1½	1.5 L	23×4
Pie Plate	8×1¼	750 mL	20×3
	9×1¼	1 L	23×3
Baking Dish or Casserole	1 quart	1 L	—
	1½ quarts	1.5 L	—
	2 quarts	2 L	—